Center Counter Defense

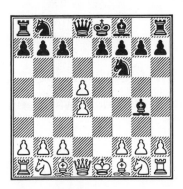

The Portuguese Variation

(1.e4 d5 2.ed5 ♞f6 3.d4 ♝g4)

Pickard
& Son
PUBLISHERS

Printed in the United States of America
ISBN: 1-886846-10-3
Cover by Statman

Center Counter Defense
The Portuguese Variation

Author: Selby Anderson
Editor: Sid Pickard

First Printing: October, 1997

Inquiries should be addressed to:

Pickard & Son, Publishers
P.O. Box 2320
Wylie, TX 75098
Tel (972) 429-9052
Fax (972) 429-9053

Contents

1.e4 d5 2.ed5 ♘f6 3.d4 ♗g4

Symbols

⩲
White has a slight advantage

⩱
Black has a slight advantage

±
White stands clearly better

∓
Black stands clearly better

+−
White is winning

−+
Black is winning

=
the game is even

#
checkmate

∞
the position is unclear

∞̿
with compensation

!
an excellent move

!!
a brilliant move

?
a mistake

??
a blunder

!?
a move deserving attention

?!
a dubious move

△
with the idea

◠
better is

Introduction

The Center Counter, or Scandinavian Defense, has been around almost from the beginning of modern chess some five hundred years ago. The characteristic moves of the original variation (1.e4 d5 2.ed5 ♕d5) took advantage of the increased reach both of the pawns and the newly empowered Queen.

The "modern" variation with 2...♘f6 gained in popularity throughout the nineteenth century, and for a brief time (c. 1910-1920) some of the world's best players added it to their repertoires, players like Capablanca, Alekhine, Rubinstein, Bogoljubow and Marshall. But the line in which White returns the pawn for a space advantage (3.d4 ♘d5) has tended to produce positions that allow White to enjoy his extra space with a minimum of complications, especially if he follows with 4.♘f3.

It is against that background that Black has tried to revive the untamed romantic possibilities of this opening with the gambit sequence **1.e4 d5 2.ed5 ♘f6 3.d4 ♗g4!?**.

Black's provocative last move probably has a long and glorious history in coffeehouse practice. It did not appear regularly in modern tournaments until the late 1980s, when the Belgian masters Pascal Vandevoort and Michel Jadoul worked out many of the key ideas.

A watershed for this variation was the success in the mid-1980s of the newly respectable Icelandic gambit (1.e4 d5 2.ed5 ♘f6 3.c4 e6 4.de6 ♗e6 – see Chapter Five). It was only a short conceptual leap to extend that idea to such lines as 3.d4 ♗g4 4.f3 ♗f5 5.c4 e6!, or 5.♗b5 ♘bd7 6.c4 e6!.

The move 3...♗g4 was warmly embraced by Portuguese IMs such as Rui Damaso, Luis Galego and Carlos P. Santos, who put this variation on the map with some stunning successes in the early 1990s. The roster of Grandmasters who have since taken up this defense on occasion includes Spraggett, Hodgson, Shirov and Hebden.

The persistent appeal of the Center Counter has been the simplicity of its concepts and rapid, economical development. The likelihood of opposite-wing castling (Black often goes Queenside) has long attracted attacking players.

As a practical matter, I believe the Portuguese variation is particularly suited to the needs of lower rated players who are playing up. The higher rated player is likely to react with disdain for this "coffeehouse" move, and seek a sharp refutation over the board. And that is exactly what Black wants!

On the other hand, if you are the higher rated player with Black you should consider that the virtues of this opening – clean lines and simplicity of concept – can work against you if your opponent is not dead set on winning. There are quiet continuations available to White where the position loses it's fizz, and Black cannot fall back on positional complexities that persist with defenses like the Sicilian or Pirc. However, for variety this opening

can spice up anyone's repertoire against 1.e4.

It is only fair to warn the reader that White has at his disposal a move order (3.♘f3 – see Chapter Five) against which there is nothing better for Black than to transpose to one of the two historic main lines with 3...♛d5 or 3...♘d5. I have no intention to retrace the mountains of accumulated theory in these variations, and I refer the reader to other sources, of which there are many.

This volume is the first systematic survey of the Portuguese variation, and contains more "virgin" analysis than is normally found in opening monographs. In some cases this reliance on original analysis results from a dearth of good material – but then, this variation has only been popular in the last ten years!

An important collaborator in this project has been artificial intelligence, specifically *Chess Machine* and *Fritz4*. That admission will undoubtedly be a turn-off to some, who may be unaware that Kasparov used *Fritz* to help prepare openings for his world championship match with Anand in 1995 (especially the spectacular Open Ruy Lopez in game 10). To me such collaboration is creative and synergistic, and can only enrich the chess world. Besides, would you contract the construction of a bridge to an engineer who refused to work with an electronic calculator? Granted, it would be hard to find such an engineer.

Onward!

After the characteristic moves **1.e4 d5 2.ed5 ♘f6 3.d4 ♗g4**, there are four main approaches for White:

Chapter Five deals with alternatives to White's 3.d4, including the 3.c4 e6 Icelandic gambit (found wanting!). Here we consider the other fourth moves:

→ A) 4.♕d3
→ B) 4.♘e2

A) 4.♕d3(?) This is an illogical move that does nothing to alleviate Black's coming d-file pressure. White's Queen sticks out like a sore thumb, obstructing develop-ment while drawing fire from all directions.

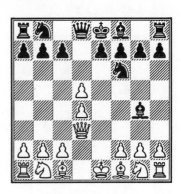

After **4...♕d5 5.♘c3** Black has two good options:

→ A1) 5...♕h5
→ A2) 5...♕d7(!)

A1) 5...♕h5 Allowing White to force a rather colorless endgame with 6.♕b5(!). If Black wants a draw this is no drawback (if you'll pardon my "punnish"). On the other hand, **6.♘ge2?! ♘c6 7.a3 0-0-0 8.♗e3 e5 9.♘g3 ♕g6 10.♕g6 hg6 11.de5 ♘e5 ∓** left Black better mobilized in Ferkingstad–D.Ribeiro, Herculane 1994.

A2) 5...♕d7(!) This move is more ambitious. Now quiet play by White would let Black seize the initiative with simple moves (e.g. ...♘c6, ...0-0-0 and ...e5). White has a dangerous pawn sacrifice, how-

ever, with **6.♘f3 ♘c6 7.♘e5!**
♛d4 8.♘c6 ♛d3 9.♗d3 bc6
10.♗f4 0-0-0 11.f3

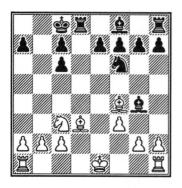

Now Os.Garcia–Sariego, Matanzas 1995 continued 11...♗h5? 12.0-0-0 ♚b8 13.♗a6 ♘d7 14.♘e4 e6 15.♖d3 ♗e7, when White could have obtained the advantage with 16.♖b3 ♘b6 17.c4! (17.a4 ♖d5!) 17...c5 18.a4 ±. However, after **11...♗d7!** White does not have enough compensation for the pawn following **12.0-0-0 e6 13.♗a6 ♚b8 14.♘a4 ♘d5 15.♖d3!? ♗c8! ∓.**

B) 4.♘e2!? was tried in Shmatkov–Ulko, Russian Ch. 1995.

(see next diagram)

Here Black can choose between two comfortable moves:

→ B1) 4...♘d5
→ B2) 4...♛d5

After 4.♘e2!?

The second, B2) 4...♛d5, is typical of the Portuguese. In the game mentioned, Black probably smelled a rat and continued with the B1) 4...♘d5 sidestep.

B1) 4...♘d5!? 5.c4 ♘b6 6.♘bc3 e5! A standard counterthrust in this opening. Not 6...♘c4?? 7.♛a4 +-. **7.c5!?** Safer is 7.f3 ♗e6 8.d5 (8.c5 ♘d5 =) 8...♗f5 9.♘g3 ♗g6 10.♗e3 ♘8d7 =. **7...♘6d7 8.♛b3** This is a situation familiar to those who have defended the 3...♘d5 4.c4 line! **8...ed4 9.♘e4** Or 9.♛b7 ♘c5 10.♛a8 ♘d3 11.♚d2 dc3 12.♚c3 ♘f2 -+. **9...♘c6 10.♗g5 ♘c5 11.♘c5 ♛g5 12.♛b7 ♛c5 13.♛a8 ♚d7 14.f3 ♛e5! 15.0-0-0 g6 16.♛b7**, and now instead of 16...♗f5 17.♛b3!, Black could have pressed a winning attack with **16...♗e6! -+.**

1.e4 d5 2.ed5 ♘f6 3.d4 ♗g4

B2) 4...♛d5 5.f3 ♝f5 Now we have:

→ **B21) 6.♘g3?!**
→ **B22) 6.♘f4**
→ **B23) 6.♘bc3**

B21) 6.♘g3?! Plausible, but after **6...♝g6 7.c4 ♛d7 8.♘c3 ♘c6 9.♝e3 0-0-0 10.d5 ♘b4 11.♖c1 e6 12.a3 ed5!** Black stands a little better.

B22) 6.♘f4 The greater danger comes from White using his Kingside pawn mass in concert with this Knight. **6...♛d6!**

To permit counterplay with ...e5. Not 6...♛d7?! 7.g4 ♝g6 8.h4 ± wrecking Black's pawns. **7.g4 ♝g6 8.h4 e5! 9.♛e2** Black also has good counterplay with 9.de5 ♛e5 10.♝e2 ♘c6 11.h5 ♖d8 ∓. **9...♛d4 10.h5 ♝c2 11.♛c2 ♝b4! ∓.**

B23) 6.♘bc3 ♛d7 7.g4 ♝g6 8.h4 h6 Also 8...h5 9.♘f4!? hg4 10.♘g6 fg6 11.♝d3 ♛e6 12.♚f1 ♘h5 13.♖g1 g3 ∞. **9.♘f4 ♝h7 10.♝b5 c6 11.♝c4 b5 12.♝b3 e6 13.a3 ♘a6 14.♛e2 ♘c7** and Black has a solid position typical of the Caro-Kann.

Now we begin our discussion of the Portuguese proper. Let us see how Black fares against more challenging White plans!

Chapter One
The Quiet 4.♗e2

1.e4 d5 2.ed5 ♘f6 3.d4 ♗g4 4.♗e2

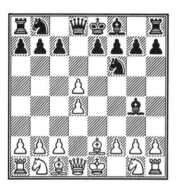

A quiet continuation whose chief appeal is simplicity and rapid development. Even so, Black frequently reaches a position with opposite side castling that gives him excellent attacking chances. Paradoxically, it appears that White's goals in this line – quiet development with a space advantage – are better served by the *zwieschenzug* 4.♗b5 ♘bd7, and only then 5.♗e2! (see Chapter Four). The reason is that Black's troublesome piece activity based on ...♕d5 and ...♘c6 is short-circuited, and the tempo "sacrificed" is used to induce a less than optimal mode of development by Black. Nevertheless, 4.♗e2 is a popular choice with which Black should be familiar.

After **4...♗e2** we consider:

➡ A) 5.♘e2
➡ B) 5.♕e2

A) **5.♘e2** Popular but wrongheaded. White follows the natural impulse to develop a minor piece and prepare castling, but this square is hardly optimal for the Knight. Also, the Queen is left on the d-file where Black quickly brings pressure to bear in the Portuguese. White can hope for no more than equality with best play. **5...♕d5** Also 5...♘d5 6.0-0 e6 7.c4 ♘b6 8.a3!? ♗e7 9.♗e3 0-0 10.♕c2 ± was Ioannides–Conlon, Britain 1994. **6.0-0**

Play divides according to Black's choice between the following two moves:

→ **A1) 6...e6**

→ **A2) 6...♘c6**

A1) 6...e6 The less enterprising of Black's two choices, this solid move may be used to steer for a setup similar to the Caro-Kann or Rubinstein French. **7.♘c3** Others are also equal, e.g. 7.♕d3 ♘c6 8.c4 ♕e4 =; 7.♗f4 c6 8.♕d3 ♘bd7 = (R.Pastor–I.Alvarez, Spanish Team Ch. 1994); 7.♘d2 c5 8.dc5 ♗c5 9.♘c3 ♕f5 10.♘b3 0-0 11.♘c5 ♕c5 = in Benev–Vandevoort, Arnheim 1987. After the text we have:

A11) 7...♕c6 8.♘f4 ♗d6 9.d5 ♕c4 10.♕f3 e5 11.b3 ♕c5 12.♘fe2 ♘bd7 13.♘g3 ♘b6 14.♖d1 ♕b4 15.h3 0-0-0 16.a3 ♕h4 17.♘f5 ♕h5 = was Mortensen–L.Meyer, Danish Team Ch. 1995.

A12) 7...♕d7 8.♗e3 If 8.♗g5 ♗e7 9.♕d3 ♘c6 10.a3 0-0-0 11.♖fd1 e5 = as in Calogridis–Chalker, Texas Open 1996. **8...♘c6 9.♕d2 ♗d6 10.♘b5 a6 11.♘d6 ♕d6 12.♖fe1 0-0-0 13.♖ad1 h5 14.♗f4 ♕d5 15.b3 ♘e4 16.♕c1 g5 17.♗e3 h4 18.c4 ♕f5 19.d5 ed5 20.cd5 ♖d5 21.♖d5 ♕d5 22.♖d1 ♕f5 23.f3** was Trbojevic–Ribeiro,

Herculane 1994 (by transposition). Black could have continued **23...♘d6 =**.

A2) 6...♘c6!

Black prepares ...0-0-0 with immediate pressure on the d4 pawn, and keeps open the option of playing ...e5 in one stroke. White can choose between:

→ **A21) 7.b3**

→ **A22) 7.♘bc3**

→ **A23) 7.c3**

A21) 7.b3 Preparing c2-c4, but White's development is too slow. **7...0-0-0 8.c4** Instead 8.♗b2 e6(?) 9.c4 ♕h5 10.♘d2 ♗d6 11.♘f3 e5 12.♘g3 gave White good play in Polovnikova–Coventry, World Cadet Ch. 1996. Black can improve, however, with 8...♕h5! (△ 9...e5) and if 9.c4 ♘d4! =. **8...♕h5** Black stands better, seen in the next diagram.

For example:

→ **A211) 9.♗b2**
→ **A212) 9.♗e3**
→ **A213) 9.♘bc3**

A211) 9.♗b2 can be answered with **9...♘d4! 10.♘d4 10.♗d4 e5. 10...♕d1 11.♖d1 e5**, and Black keeps his extra pawn because of White's awkward piece placement. Note that if his Queen's Bishop were on e3, White would have **12.♘c3 =**.

A212) 9.♗e3 e5! 10.d5 ♘g4 11.h3 ♘e3 12.fe3 ♗c5 Again, Black wins a pawn by force. **13.♖f3 e4 14.♖g3 ♘e7! 15.b4 ♗b4 16.♖g4 ♘f5 17.♖e4 ♘g3!** −+. Gayson–Bryson, British National Club Ch. 1997.

A213) 9.♘bc3 e6 Or 9...♘d4 10.♘d4 ♕d1 11.♖d1 e5 12.♗e3 =. **10.♗b2 ♗d6 11.h3 ♖hg8** A

recurring theme: Black develops a strong Kingside attack based on ...g5-g4. **12.♘b5 ♗e7 13.♕d3 g5 14.♘g3 ♕h4 15.♘e2 a6 16.♘a3 g4 17.♕g3 ♕h6 18.♔h1 ♗a3 19.♗a3 ♘d4 20.♗c1 ♕h5 21.♘c3 ♘f5 22.♕f4 gh3 23.g3 ♖d3 24.♖g1 ♖g4**, 0-1 (25.♕e5 ♘g3) was Agosto–A.Carvalho, World Junior Ch. 1995.

A22) 7.♘bc3 Consistent with White's plan of rapid, straightforward development. The problem is that his d-pawn is vulnerable. We consider three replies:

→ **A221) 7...♕d7**
→ **A222) 7...♕h5**
→ **A223) 7...♕f5**

A221) 7...♕d7?! This dilutes the effect of a later ...0-0-0, which is always psychologically unpleasant to White when a Rook is "smiling" at his Queen. **8.d5!** For 8.♗e3 =, see A1) 6...e6. **8...♘b4 9.♘f4 g6** Alternatives are no better: 9...0-0-0 10.♕d4! ♘fd5 11.♘cd5 ♘d5 12.♕a7 ♘b6 13.♗e3 ±, or 9...g5 10.a3 ♘c2 11.♕c2 gf4 12.♗f4 ♗g7 13.♖ac1 ±. **10.a3 ♘a6 11.♗e3 ♗g7 12.♕e2 0-0 13.♖ad1** White has a large advantage in space and in piece coordination. Vogt–Kassenbaum, Germany 1995 continued **13...♘e8 14.♘b5! ♘d6 15.c4 ♘f5 16.b4 b6 17.♖fe1 ♖fe8 18.♕f3 ♘b8 19.♘d4 ♘e3 20.♖e3 a5 21.d6 cd6 22.♕a8 ♗d4 23.♖d4 ♘c6 24.♖d6!, 1-0**.

A222) 7...♕h5

Now on **8.♘f4?!** Black can respond with **8...♕f5 △ 9...g5**. Little better was **8.♗f4 0-0-0 9.a4 e5 10.♗g3 a6 11.♘a2 ed4 12.♕d3 ♗d6 ∓** in Huda–A.Carvalho, Yerevan Olympiad 1996. Otherwise two moves have been seen:

➙ **A2221) 8.d5**
➙ **A2222) 8.♗e3**

A2221) 8.d5 0-0-0 9.♘f4 ♕f5 If **9...♕d1 10.♖d1 ♘b4 11.♖d2 △ a3**. **10.♕e2 ♘b4 11.♗e3 g5 12.♘h3 ♘bd5 13.♘g5 ♖g8 14.♘d5 ♘d5 15.♘f3 e6 16.♖ad1 ♗d6 17.c4 ♕h5 18.g3**

♘f6 19.♔g2 ♘g4 20.h3 ♘e5 21.c5 ♗e7 22.♘d4 ♕e2 23.♘e2 ♘d3 24.c6 was played in Camilleri–Warner, Yerevan Olympiad 1996. Now **24...b6! 25.b3 ♘b4 ∓** is clearly in Black's favor.

A2222) 8.♗e3 0-0-0 9.♕d3 Enticing Black to play 9...♘b4? when 10.♕c4 is strong. **9...e5** Playable is 9...♘g4, when De Vuyst–Joseph, 1989 continued 10.h3 (10.♗f4? e5!) 10...♘e3 11.fe3!? (11.♕e3 =) 11...e5 12.♕e4 (12.♖f5 ♕g6 13.♖af1 f6 14.♕c4 ♔b8 =) 12...f6 13.d5 ♘b4 14.♘g3 ♕g6 15.♘f5 ♕f7 16.♖ad1 g6 17.♘g3 f5, and now White sacrificed his Knight unsoundly on f5. The alternative was 18.♕e5 ♗c5! 19.♕f4 ♘c2 20.♖f3 ♖he8 21.♔f2 ♕e7 22.♘f1 ♔b8! △ 23...g5 with good play for Black. **10.♖ad1** Or 10.d5? ♘b4 ∓; 10.♘g3 ♕g6 11.♕g6 hg6 12.de5 ♘g4! ∓. **10...♘g4 11.h3 ♘e3 12.fe3 ed4 13.♖f5** Not 13.ed4? ♘d4! winning a pawn, the point being 14.♘d4?? ♖d4 15.♕d4 ♗c5 −+. On 13.♘b5 best is 13...♗e7! (13...de3?? 14.♘a7! +−) 14.♘bd4 (14.ed4? a6 15.♘bc3 ♘d4) 14...♗f6 ∓. **13...♕g6 14.ed4 ♗d6** and Black is equal or slightly better.

A223) 7...♕f5 A finesse, to lure White into playing ♘g3. This would remove the Knight from the defense of the d-pawn, and expose him to h5-h4 attacking on the Kingside with tempo. **8.♘g3 ♕d7 9.♗e3 0-0-0 10.♘ce2 h5! 11.f3**

Anchoring a central flight square for the Knight. Belo–Liardet, World Universities Ch. 1996 continued instead 11.♖e1?! h4 12.♘f1 h3 13.♘f4 (Or 13.g3 g5! 14.c4 ♘e5! 15.♘d2 ♘c4! ∓) 13...hg2 14.♘g2 ♘d4 and White eventually lost the ending. Also unsatisfactory is 11.h4 ♕g4! 12.c4!? ♕h4 13.♕a4 ♘g4 14.♖fd1 ♕h2 15.♔f1 h4 16.d5 ♘b8! and Black's attack will continue at no risk to his own King. The text (which came to my attention in a blitz game with a Class A player in San Antonio, Ernie Shown) manages to keep White in the game. Black has two good continuations from the last

diagram – one "solid" and one "sharp."

A2231) 11...e5 A perfectly natural and correct move. **12.c3 ♘d5 13.♗f2 f5** 13...h4 14.♘e4 f5 15.♘g5 ♖h5 16.♘h3 g5. **14.de5 h4 15.♘h1 ♕e8 16.♕c2 ♕e5 17.f4 ♕e6 18.♘d4 ♘d4 19.♗d4 ♖e8 =.**

A2232) 11...♕e6!? Played to take away the e4 flight square from White's Knight at g3 – hence White's reply. A sharp tactical skirmish follows, which probably levels out with best play. **12.♕d3 ♘b4 13.♘f4 ♕c6 14.♕b3 h4 15.♘ge2 g5 16.♘d3 ♘d3 17.♗g5!** 17.♕d3 g4 ∓. **17...h3 18.g3 ♘b4 19.♕b4 ♕c2 20.♖f2 ♘d5 21.♕a3 ♔b8 22.♖c1 ♕f5 23.f4 f6 24.♗h4 e5** ∞.

A23) 7.c3 0-0-0 8.♘f4 By securing the center, White finds a use for his e2 Knight and allows his Queen to venture out to a4. However, Black's greater economy of development soon becomes clear. **8...♕d6** Or 8...♕f5 9.♕d3 ♕d3 10.♘d3 e5 11.♘e5 ♘e5 12.de5 ♘g4 13.♗f4 ♗c5 = in Papazov–Vescovi, World Cadet Ch. 1995.

1.e4 d5 2.ed5 ♘f6 3.d4 ♗g4

Black has adequate compensation for the pawn. **9.♕a4 e5**

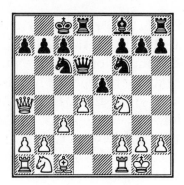

10.de5 On 10.♘e2 ed4 11.♖d1 ♘g4 12.♗f4 ♕f6 13.cd4 ♗d6, Black stands much better. **10...♕e5 11.♘d2 ♗c5 12.♘f3 ♕f5 13.♘e2** If 13.b4 ♗b6 (13...♗d6 14.b5 ♘b8 isn't bad either) 14.c4 ♕e4! 15.♕b3 ♘d4 16.♘d4 ♗d4 17.♖b1 ♘g4! with the unpleasant threat of 18...♘f2!, e.g. 18.♘h3 (Or 18.♘d3 ♕d3! 19.♕d3 ♗f2 ∓) 18...♗e5 19.f3 ♕e2! 20.♗f4 ♗f4 21.♘f4 ♕e3 22.♕e3 ♘e3 wins a pawn. **13...♖he8** Black tried a speculative pawn sac in Kurcubic–Liardet, World Universities Ch. 1996, but 13...♕d3 14.♘g3 ♘d5 (14...♖he8 15.♗g5) 15.♕g4 ♔b8 16.♕g7 f6 17.♕g4 h5 followed, when 18.♕e4! ♕a6 19.♖d1 would have been favorable to White. **14.♘g3 ♕g4! 15.♕g4 ♘g4 16.♗f4 h6 17.h3 ♘ge5 18.♘e5 ♘e5 19.♗e5** Otherwise ...♘d3 is trou-

blesome. **19...♖e5** Black may have a sliver of an advantage in the endgame due to his strong Bishop.

B) 5.♕e2 This is clearly White's best recapture, to vacate the vulnerable d-file, support c2-c4, and develop the King's Knight to its natural f3 square. After **5...♕d5 6.♘f3** Black has two responses in the following position:

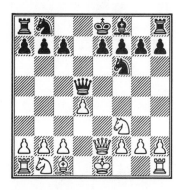

→ **B1) 6...♘c6**
→ **B2) 6...e6!**

B1) 6...♘c6 Here this natural developing move is problematic because of the thrust **7.c4** The less challenging moves 7.0-0 and 7.♗e3 transpose to B2) 6...e6. Note that after 7.0-0, capturing the the d-pawn is a mistake: 7...♘d4? 8.♘d4 ♕d4 9.♕b5 ±. Instead Black should play 7...0-0-0. Another seventh move, featuring a trap which nabbed a GM, is 7.♘c3 ♕h5 8.♗g5? ♘d4! −+ as in Svidler–

Shirov, 1996. Better is 8.0-0 0-0-0 9.Ξd1 e6 = transposing into Campora–Spraggett, Spain 1996 – again see B2) 6...e6.

After 7.c4 the move 7...$\mathbb{W}$h5? is met by 8.d5 $\triangle$b4 9.a3 $\triangle$a6 10.b4! with a big space advantage to White, so we have:

→ **B11) 7...$\mathbb{W}$e4**
→ **B12) 7...$\mathbb{W}$f5**

B11) 7...$\mathbb{W}$e4

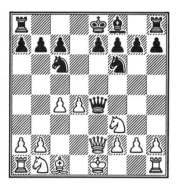

Simplification alone fails to neutralize White's space advantage in the center and Queenside. Two possibilities:

B111) 8.$\triangle$c3 $\mathbb{W}$e2 9.$\triangle$e2 e6 10.0-0 0-0-0 11.$\triangle$f4 $\triangle$d6 12.$\triangle$d6 cd6 13.Ξab1 d5 14.c5 $\triangle$e4 15.Ξfd1 f6 16.$\triangle$d2 $\triangle$g5 17.h4 $\triangle$f7 18.$\triangle$f1 e5 19.$\triangle$e3 $\triangle$e7 20.b4 ± was Bruneau–Collas, Hyeres 1992. White eventually broke through with b5, Ξdc1, a4-a5, c6 and b6.

B112) 8.$\triangle$e3!? e5 9.d5 $\triangle$b4 10.0-0 Or 10.$\triangle$c3 as in M. Badals–Fioramonti, Horgen 1994 when Black should have played 10...$\triangle$c2! 11.$\dot{\triangle}$d1 (11.$\dot{\triangle}$d2 $\triangle$b4!) 11...$\triangle$e3 12.fe3 $\mathbb{W}$f5 13.e4 $\mathbb{W}$h5 14.$\triangle$b5 $\dot{\triangle}$d8 =. **10...$\mathbb{W}$d3 11.Ξe1 $\triangle$g4 12.$\triangle$d4 f6 13.h3 $\triangle$h6** Black has a solid position.

B12) 7...$\mathbb{W}$f5 Black prepares to meet d4-d5 with ...$\triangle$b4, pressuring the c2 and d3 squares. White therefore gains nothing by 8.d5 $\triangle$b4 9.$\triangle$d4 $\triangle$d3 10.$\dot{\triangle}$d2 $\triangle$c1 11.$\mathbb{W}$e7 $\triangle$e7 12.$\triangle$f5 $\triangle$c5 13.Ξe1 $\dot{\triangle}$f8 14.$\dot{\triangle}$c1 $\triangle$f2 15.Ξe2 $\triangle$b6 with an equal ending. White may try instead:

→ **B121) 8.0-0**
→ **B122) 8.a3**

B121) 8.0-0 divides further:

B1211) 8...e6 White now gets a comfortable space advantage after 9.$\triangle$e3 $\triangle$d6 (9...0-0-0 10.a3 ±) 10.$\triangle$c3 0-0 11.Ξad1 Ξfe8 (Atlas-Hodgson, 1996) 12.Ξfe1 Ξad8 ± (Atlas). The attempt to squeeze more from the position with **9.d5!? $\triangle$b4** only muddies the situation because White is not sufficiently developed:

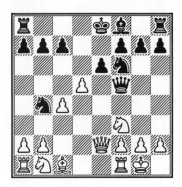

B12111) 10.de6 ♘c2! 11.ef7 ♔f7 12.♘e5 ♔g8 13.c5 h6 ∓. On the other hand, 10...0-0-0 11.e7 ♗e7 12.♕e7 ♘c2, which looks convincing, is thwarted by 13.♕e5!, assuring that White will trap the Knight after it captures the a1 Rook: 13...♕e5 (13...♕d3 14.♗f4) 14.♘e5 ♖hf8 15.♘a3 ♘a1 16.♗e3 ±, and possibly ±.

B12112) 10.a3 ♘c2 11.♖a2 (±, Atlas) 11...♗c5! 12.de6 12.♖d1 ♘g4!. 12...fe6 13.b4 ♘d4 14.♘d4 ♗d4 15.♗e3 0-0-0 16.♖d2 e5 and Black has no difficulties.

B1212) 8...0-0-0 9.♗e3 9.d5 ♘b4 10.♘d4 (10.♘e1 e6 11.a3 ♘a6 12.de6 ♘c5! ∓) 10...♕d3 leads to an equal endgame: 11.a3 ♕e2 12.♘e2 ♘d3 13.b4 ♘c1 14.♖c1 g6 15.♘bc3 ♗h6 16.♖d1 ♖he8 17.♖ab1 e6 18.de6 ♖e6

19.♖d8 ♔d8 20.♖d1 (Ratcu-A.Carvalho, Duisburg 1992) 20...♔e8 21.♘d4 ♖e7 =. **9...e6** Instead 9...e5!? 10.d5 ♘b4 puts the Queen's Knight out of play after 11.♘e1! ♗d6, and either 12.♘c3 or 12.a3 ♘a6 13.b4 e4 (△ 14...♕e5) 14.♗d4! gives White an advantage. **10.♘c3**

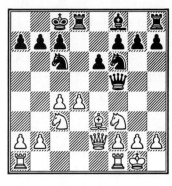

Interesting is 10.a3 to get the Queenside rolling. After the text move Black obtained counterplay with **10...g5!?** in Jojic–Patrat, Paris 1990 following 11.♖ad1(?) ♖g8 12.a3 g4 13.♘h4 ♕a5, when White's thrust b2-b4 is hindered. More logical is 11.♖fd1 ♖g8 12.a3 g4 13.♘h4 ♕h5 14.g3, or even the pawn grab **11.♘g5(!) ♘d4 12.♗d4 ♖d4 13.♘f7 ♖g8 14.♖ae1**, with the fantastic possibility **14...♘d7 15.♘e5 ♘e5 16.♕e5 ♖g2 17.♔g2 ♖g4 18.♔h3! ♕f3 19.♕g3! ±.**

B122) 8.a3 g6 Failures include 8...e6 9.d5 ±, 8...♕g4!? 9.d5 ♘a5 10.♘bd2 b5 11.cb5 ♘d5 12.g3 △ 13.b4 and 14.♗b2 ±, and 8...0-0-0? – which is not a serious option because of 9.d5 ♘a5 10.♘bd2 followed by 11.b4, and Black will soon be obliged to play the weakening ...b6 to save his Knight. **9.♘c3** The plausible 9.b4 ♗g7 10.♗b2 runs afoul of 10...♘h5! 11.0-0 (11.g3 0-0-0) 11...♘f4 12.♕e3 ♕g4 13.g3 ♘e6, and Black stands better. **9...♗g7 10.0-0** White cannot go after the c7 pawn just yet: 10.♘b5 0-0 11.♘c7?? ♕a5 and 12...♕c7. **10...♖d8 11.♘b5!** In Carvalho–Gomez Esteban, Moscow Olympiad 1994, White played too passively and got into trouble with 11.♖d1 0-0 12.h3 e6 13.♗e3 ♖d7 14.♖d2 ♖fd8 15.♖ad1 ♘e4! 16.♘e4 ♕e4, and neither 17.♕d3 ♕d3 18.♖d3 e5 ∓ nor the game continuation 17.♗g5 ♕e2 18.♖e2 ♘d4! ∓ is satisfactory for White. After the text, White gains a decided edge, e.g. **11...0-0** 11...♖d7? 12.d5, △ 13.♘e5. **12.d5 ♘a5 13.♗e3 ♕g4 14.♖ac1 c6 15.h3 ♕f5 16.♘bd4!,** △ 17.♗d2 ±.

In summary, the lines with 6...♘c6 give White a space advantage without setting up sufficient chances for a Kingside counterattack.

B2) 6...e6

The coming rapid deployment of ...♗d6, in combination with ...♕h5 (if provoked), ...♘c6 and an eventual ...g5, gives Black excellent chances of striking a blow on the Kingside. White has played:

→ **B21) 7.♗f4**
→ **B22) 7.0-0**
→ **B23) 7.c4(!)**

The move 7.♘c3 transposes after 7...♕h5 8.0-0 to <u>B22) 7.0-0</u> below.

B21) 7.♗f4 This move can lead to tame equality after 7...♗d6 8.♘c3 ♕a5. More enterprising for Black is **7...♘c6!?** **8.♘c3** 8.♗c7 ♘d4 9.♘d4 ♕d4 10.♗b5 ♕d7 =. **8...♕a5 9.0-0 0-0-0** 9...♗d6. **10.♖fd1** 10.♘b5 a6!. **10...♕f5 11.♗g3 ♗d6 12.♗d6 cd6** =. To be avoided, however, is 7...c5?! when Black was blown out of the water in Mosquera–Cukier, 1996 after **8.♘c3 ♕c6 9.♘e5 ♕b6 10.♘c4 ♕a6 11.d5 b5 12.♘b5 ♘d5 13.0-0-0 ♘f4 14.♘c7 ♔e7 15.♕d2 ♘e2 16.♔b1 ♘c3 17.♕c3 ♕c6 18.♘a8 ♕a8 19.♕e5 f6 20.♕c7, 1-0.**

B22) 7.0-0 Reaching the position shown below.

Black can now choose between:

→ **B221) 7...♘c6**
→ **B222) 7...♗d6**

B221) 7...♘c6 Instead 7...♗e7 8.c4 ♕f5 is <u>B23) 7.c4</u>. After the text we examine three moves for White. In all cases, Black is holding his own.

→ **B2211) 8.♖d1**
→ **B2212) 8.♘c3**
→ **B2213) 8.♗e3**

B2211) 8.♖d1 0-0-0 White has a safe position, nothing more. There may follow **9.c4** Or 9.♘c3 ♕h5 10.♗f4 ♗d6 11.♗d6 ♖d6 12.♖d2 ♖hd8 13.♖ad1 a6 14.h3 g5 15.♕e3 h6 16.♘e5 ♘e5 17.♕e5 ♕g6 = in Campora–Spraggett, Spain 1996. **9...♕h5 10.♘c3 ♗d6** 10...♖g8 11.♗e3 g5 12.d5 g4 13.♘d2 ed5 14.cd5 ♗d6 15.♘f1 ♘e5 16.♔h1 ♘f3 17.g3 = Ranola–Cukier, PHI-BRA match 1995. **11.c5** 11.a3 e5 12.d5 e4 13.♘e4 ♗h2 ∓ was Kouwenhoven–Hodgson, 1996. **11...♗e7 12.b4 e5 13.de5 ♖d1 14.♘d1 ♘g4 15.♗f4 ♕f5 16.♗g3 ♖d8 17.h3 ♘h6 18.b5 ♘b4 19.♕c4 ♕c2 20.♕c2 ♘c2 21.♖c1 ♘f5,** 1/2-1/2. Zulfugarli–Forster, World Collegiate Ch. 1996.

B2212) 8.♘c3 ♕f5 9.♘b5 Black has nothing to fear from this sortie. **9...0-0-0!?** Or 9...♗d6 10.c4 0-0, and a draw was agreed in in Ochoa de Echaguen–Sariego, 1993. **10.♘e5 ♘d4 11.♘d4 ♖d4 12.♘f7 ♖g8 13.♘g5 ♗d6 14.♕e6 ♕e6 15.♘e6 ♖e4 16.♘g5 ♖e2** ⯑ was Hauchard–Vandevoort, Paris 1990.

B2213) 8.♗e3 0-0-0 9.c4 ♕h5 10.♘c3 ♖g8 11.♖fd1 g5

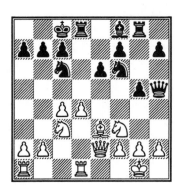

Similar positions can arise with Black's Queen on f5 in <u>B12) 7...♕f5</u> above. **12.d5** Once seen was 12.♘e5 ♕e2 13.♘e2 ♘e5 14.de5 ♖d1 15.♖d1 ♘g4 16.♗d4 (L.Sepulveda–G.Carvalho, Women's Olympiad 1994) 16...♗g7 17.♗a7 ♘e5 18.♗d4 ♘c4 ∓. **12...g4 13.dc6 gf3 14.♖d8 ♔d8** So far as in Grebennikov–Ulko, Moscow 1994 when White's game quickly went south: 15.♕d1?? ♗d6 16.g3 ♘g4 17.h4 ♘e3 18.cb7 ♔e7 19.♕b3 ♕h4, 0-1. Instead, White has to play **15.♕d3 ♗d6 16.g3 ♕h3** 16...♘g4 17.h4 b6 18.♗f4 ±. **17.♕f1 ♕f1 18.♖f1 b6 19.♘b5 ♔e7** with equal endgame chances.

B222) 7...♗d6 The characteristic move of the <u>B2) 6...e6</u> line. White has played one of the three following responses:

→ **B2221) 8.c4**
→ **B2222) 8.♘c3**
→ **B2223) 8.♗g5**

B2221) 8.c4(?) As natural as it looks, this space-gaining move is misplaced after 7.0-0 because Black can quickly stir up an attack with simple moves. I recommend <u>B23) 7.c4</u> if White's intention is to push the c-pawn. **8...♕h5** Threatening 9...♗h2. **9.♘c3 ♘c6** And now Black threatens 10...♘d4! −+. **10.h3** Something has gone wrong if White has to weaken his Kingside thus. But the alternative 10.♗e3 only postpones this ugly necessity for one move after 10...g5!, when 11.h3 transposes to our main line, and 11.g3 ♘g4! 12.♖fd1 0-0-0 likewise gave Black a good attacking game in F.Costa–P.Lima, Loures Young Masters 1996: 13.a3 ♖hg8 14.♔g2 f5 15.b4 e5 16.h3 ♘e3 17.fe3 g4 ∓ 18.hg4 ♕g4 19.♕e1 ed4 20.♘e2 de3 21.b5 ♘e5 22.♘e5 ♗e5 23.♖d8 ♖d8 24.♖d1 ♖d1 25.♕d1 ♗g3 26.♕d5 f4 27.♘d4 ♗f2 28.♔f1 ♕d1 29.♔g2 ♕g1 30.♔f3 ♕h1 31.♔f4 ♕d5 32.cd5 ♔d7, 0-1. **10...0-0-0 11.♗e3 g5! 12.♘g5 ♕g6 13.♕f3 ♗b4**

(see next diagram)

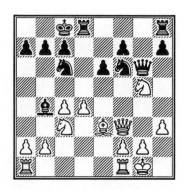

The two games from this position have been showcases for Black's attacking potential in the Portuguese:

1) **14.♖fd1 ♗c3 15.bc3 h6 16.d5 ♘e5 17.♕e2 hg5 18.♗a7 ♕f5 19.♖ab1 ♘e4 20.♗d4 g4 21.♕b2 b6 22.♕a3 gh3 23.♗b6 ♘f3! 24.♔f1 hg2 25.♔e2 ♘g3 26.fg3 ♕e4 27.♗e3 g1=♘ 28.♔f1 ♕c4 29.♔g2 ♖h2#, 0-1.** Ye–Damaso (China-Portugal match), Macao 1996.

2) **14.♖ad1 ♗c3 15.bc3 h6 16.h4 hg5 17.♗g5 ♘e4 18.♗d8 ♘d8 19.♕h3?** 19.♕d3 f5 20.d5 ed5 21.♕d5 ♘c6 ∓. Now instead of 19...f5 (1/2-1/2 in Nunn–Damaso, Oviedo rapid 1992) Black can win by force with **19...♘g5! 20.♕g3 ♖h4 21.♖fe1** 21.f4 ♘h3 22.♔h2 ♘f4 −+. **21...♕h7! 22.f3** 22.♔f1 ♖h1 23.♔e2 ♕c2

24.♖d2 ♖e1 25.♔e1 ♕d2 26.♔d2 ♘e4 −+. **22...♖h1 23.♔f2 ♕c2 24.♔e3 ♕c3 25.♔f2 ♕c2 26.♔e3 ♖e1 27.♖e1 f6 −+.**

B2222) 8.♘c3 ♕h5

9.♕b5 There is a good safe drawing line for White in 9.d5, as practice has shown: 9...♘d5 10.♕b5 ♘d7 11.♘e4 0-0-0 12.c4 ♘5f6 13.♘d6 cd6 14.♕b4 ♔b8 15.♗e3 ♘e5 16.♕c3 ♘fg4 17.♗d4 ♘c6 18.♖ad1 e5 19.h3 ♘f6, 1/2-1/2 was S.Gonzalez–Damaso, Havana 1990. **9...♕b5** Riskier is 9...♘c6!? 10.♕h5 (10.♕b7? ♘d4! ∓) 10...♘h5 11.♘b5 0-0 12.♘d6 cd6 13.c4 and White had a sliver of an edge in Echavarria–Cukier, World Junior Ch. 1996. **10.♘b5 a6 11.♘d6 cd6 12.♗f4 d5 13.a4 ♘c6 14.a5 ♖c8 15.c3 ♔e7** = was Batceceg–S.Lalic, Yerevan Olympiad 1996.

B2223) 8.♗g5 Fairly untested, but not very dangerous for either side. Waitzkin–Vitor, World Junior Ch. 1994 was drawn after **8...♕f5 9.♗f6 gf6 10.♘c3 ♘d7 11.d5 ♘e5 12.de6 ♘f3 13.♕f3 ♕f3 14.ef7 ♔f7 15.gf3 ♖hg8 16.♔h1 f5 17.♘e2 ♖ae8 18.♘g3 ♗g3 19.fg3, 1/2-1/2**.

B23) 7.c4

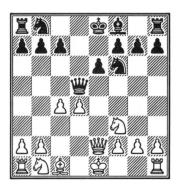

This is White's best continuation. He takes away any special tactics based on "castling into it," while keeping a modest space advantage. There may follow:

➝ **B231) 7...♕h5**
➝ **B232) 7...♕f5**

B231) 7...♕h5 8.♘c3 There is little point to 8.d5?!, e.g. 8...♗b4 9.♗d2 ♗d2 10.♘bd2 0-0 11.de6 ♖e8 when Black is a shade better than equal. Playable is 8.♗g5, although there is little practice with

this move. A likely continuation is 8...♗e7 9.♘c3 ♘bd7 10.d5 e5 11.♘e4 0-0 12.♘g3 ♗b4 13.♔f1 and White was already losing the thread in Fenton–House, IECG (Internet) 1995. **8...♗b4** On moves such as 8...♘c6 or 8...♗d6, White does not cooperate by castling (which transposes to the inferior B2221) 8.c4 line), but plays 9.d5 ±. Possible is 8...c6, when 9.d5!? cd5 10.cd5 is less dangerous than it looks: 10...♘d5 11.♕b5 ♘d7 12.♕b7 ♘5b6! 13.♗e3 ♕a5 14.0-0 ♖b8 15.♕e4 ♕b4 =. Of course, White can just maintain the status quo in the center with 9.0-0(!). **9.♗d2 0-0 10.a3 ♗c3 11.♗c3 ♘c6 12.0-0** White has a modest pull based on his space advantage. Kiik–Galego, Sas van Gent 1994 continued **12...♖fe8 13.♖fe1 a6 14.a4 ♘e7 15.a5 ♘g6 16.♕e3 h6 17.h3 ♕f5 18.♘e5 ♘e5 19.♕e5 ♕e5 20.♖e5 ±**.

B232) 7...♕f5 8.0-0 ♗e7 Instead 8...♘c6 leads to A2) 6...♘c6. **9.♘c3 0-0** Here the game took an unexpectedly sharp turn in Leko–Damaso, Yerevan Olympiad 1996.

(see next diagram)

10.d5!? ♗c5! 11.de6 ♘c6 12.♗e3 ♖ae8 Here White chose the safe

After 9...0-0

way out with 13.♗c5 ♛c5 14.ef7 ♖f7 15.♛c2 ♛c4 =. Since that idea clearly fizzled, I suggest that White instead nurse his space advantage with **10.a3 a5 11.♗g5 ♘c6 12.♖ad1 ♖ad8 13.♗h4 ♖d7 14.♖d2 ♖fd8 15.♖fd1** ±.

In summary, the lines with 4.♗e2 promise White nothing exciting unless he walks into one of the fertile attacking positions for Black. However, if White defers castling and plays an early c4 as in <u>B23) 7.c4</u>, he may get a persistent edge in space.

Chapter Two
The Sharp 4.f3

1.e4 d5 2.ed5 ♘f6 3.d4 ♗g4 4.f3

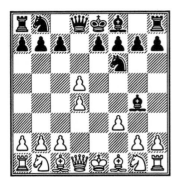

A move with attitude. White sets out to hold the gambit pawn and refute Black's opening in the most straightforward way. On the down side, 4.f3 takes away the best square for the King's Knight, and it creates a weakness at e3 which makes White vulnerable on the e-file. Black needs to open lines and scramble his pieces if he is to make good his investment of a pawn.

After **4...♗f5** White has a tempo to spend on either

→ **A) 5.c4**
→ **B) 5.♗b5**

Others include:

1) **5.g4!?** An intermezzo not to be dismissed out of hand, since the violent 5...♘g4? doesn't work. However, after **5...♗g6 6.c4 e6!** (anyway!) Black can play for rapid castling and counterplay on the f-file. For example, after 7.g5 ♘h5 8.♘c3 ♗d6 9.de6 0-0 10.ef7 ♖f7 11.♗d3 ♘c6 12.♗g6 hg6 White's King is already feeling insecure. Or **7.de6 ♗b4 8.♗d2 9.♕d2 0-0 10.g5 ♘h5 11.♗h3 ♘c6 12.♘e2 fe6 13.♗e6 ♔h8 14.0-0 ♗b1! 15.♖ab1 ♘f4 16.♘f4 ♕g5**, regaining one pawn with excellent compensation for the other, given the weakness at f3.

2) **5.♗d3** Another sideline without much practice to draw upon, this move was played in Coste–Chaplin, Paris 1990.

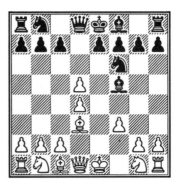

After 5...♕d5 White continued too passively: 6.♘e2 ♘c6 7.a3?! 0-0-0 8.c4 ♕d7 9.♗e3 ♘e5! and Black stood better. Instead, White should

have played 6.c4! ♕d7 7.♗f5 ♕f5 8.♕b3! ±, hitting the b-pawn before Black has a chance to finish Queenside development. He can't be too happy with the opening if he has nothing better than 8...b6. So the milk-and-water 5.♗d3 may contain some poison! Let's consider the alternative recapture **5...♗d3 6.♕d3 ♘d5** Now White would be foolish to go after the b-pawn with 7.♕b5? ♘c6 8.♕b7 ♘db4! ∓, or 8.♘e2 ♘b4! 9.♘a3 a6! 10.♕c4 e5 ∓. Better is **7.c4 ♘b4 8.♕b3 ♘8c6 9.♘e2 b5!** 10.a3 bc4 11.♕c4 ♕d5 12.♕d5 ♘d5 =. The slower 7.a3 leaves the d-pawn vulnerable after 7...♘c6 8.♘e2 ♕d7 9.c4 ♘b6 10.f4 e6 △ 11...0-0-0 ∓.

A) **5.c4** Naked materialism! With the gambit reply 5...e6, Black obtains a big lead in development – but is it enough? Our laboratory's verdict is an unequivocal "maybe."

In passing, we note that Black has tried the alternative **5...c6!? 6.dc6 ♘c6**, when best seems 7.♗e3. A game Nataf–Dias, Szeged 1994 continued **7.d5 ♘e5 8.♘c3 e6 9.g4 ♘fg4** with absurd complications:

(see next diagram)

10.♕a4 ♘d7 11.fg4 ♕h4 12.♔d1 ♕g4 13.♗e2 ♕g2 14.♗e3 ♕h1 15.♔d2 ♕h2 16.♘f3 ♕b8 17.♘d4 b5 18.♘cb5 a6 19.de6 ab5 20.ed7 ♗d7 21.♕c2 bc4 22.♕e4 ♗e7 23.♗c4 ♕b4 24.♔d3 ♖d8 25.b3 ♗b5 26.♖c1 ♔f8? 26...0-0 -+. 27.♗d2 ♗c4 28.♖c4 ♕b6 29.♔c2 ♕g6 30.♘f5 ♗a3 31.♗c3 f6 32.b4 ♕f7 33.♔b3 ♗c1 34.b5 g6 35.♗b4 ♔g8 36.♘d6 ♕d7 37.♖c1 ♔g7 38.b6 ♕h3 39.♖c3 ♕h2 40.♖c7 ♔h6 41.♗d2 ♔h5 42.♕f3 ♔h4 43.♗e1, 1-0.

Returning to **5...e6**, we may compare this plan to the Icelandic gambit (1.e4 d5 2.ed5 ♘f6 3.c4 e6 4.de6 ♗e6 – see Chapter Five), with which Black scored many successes in the 1980s predating widespread use of the Portuguese. I don't think this similarity is a coincidence! Black was probably emboldened to apply similar ideas in new situations. **6.de6 ♘c6!** Full throttle forward! Black's jump in development can take on intimidating proportions.

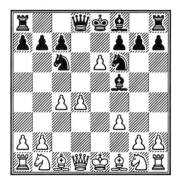

Now we consider:

→ **A1) 7.ef7?**
→ **A2) 7.♘e2?**
→ **A3) 7.d5?**
→ **A4) 7.♗e3**

A1) 7.ef7? This is really tweaking the tiger's tail. In grabbing the second pawn White ensures that the Black King's Rook will come into play while his own King is in still the center. **7...♔f7** All the evidence at hand suggests that Black is simply winning this position. Almost his entire army has been mobilized, while White is still choosing which piece will be first out of the box. We offer three samples of Black's mobility:

A11) 8.♗d3 ♗b4 9.♘c3 ♖e8 10.♘ge2 ♗d3 11.♕d3 (Stoianowski–Ribeiro, Baile Herculane 1994) and now Black wins with **11...♘d4! 12.♔f2 ♘e2 13.♕d8 ♗c5 14.♔f1** 14.♔e1 ♘g3. **14...♖ad8 −+**.

A12) 8.♗e3 ♗b4 9.♔f2 9.♘c3 ♖e8 10.♔f2 ♖e3! 11.♔e3 ♘d4 12.♕d4 ♕e7 −+, △ 13.♔f4? ♘h5 14.♔f5 ♕e6 15.♔g5 ♗e7 16.♔h5 ♕g6#. **9...♖e8**

10.♘c3 10.♘e2 ♖e3 11.♔e3 ♕e7 12.♔f2 ♖e8 13.♕c1 ♘d4! 14.♘d4 ♗e1 15.♔g1 ♕c5 16.♕d1 ♗c2!, 0-1 was Dimitrov–Rivera, Lalin 1994. **10...♖e3 11.♔e3 ♕e7 12.♔f2 ♘d4 13.♕e1 ♕c5 14.♔g3** 14.♕e3 ♘c2 −+. **14...♘h5, 0-1** as in R.Hess–Chalker, Houston 1995 (15.♔h4 ♕e7! leads to mate).

A13) 8.d5 ♘b4 9.♘a3 ♗c5 10.♗e2 ♖e8 11.♔f1 ♕e7

12.♗g5 h6 13.♗f6 13.♗h4
♛e3!, △ ...g5 and ...♘h5 −+.
13...♛f6 14.♛d2 ♖e7 15.g4
15.♛c3 ♛c3 16.bc3 ♘d3; 15.f4
♖ae8. **15...♗g4 16.♘b5** 16.h3
♖e2 17.♛e2 ♖e8 18.♛g2 ♗f5 −+.
So far as in Meyer–S.Young, Texas
Open 1995, where Black missed a
win with **16...♗e3! 17.♛e1**
17.♛b4 ♛h4 −+; 17.♛d1 ♛h4
18.♛e1 ♗h3 or 18...♛h3 and mate
next. **17...♘c2 18.♛g3 ♗f4!**
19.♛g4 19.♛f2 ♘e3 20.♔e1 ♛b2
−+. **19...♘e3 −+.**

A2) 7.♘e2? This obscure move
puts the rule of thumb "Knights before Bishops" ahead of common
sense. **7...♘b4!** The most ambitious reply. Shirov played 7...fe6
against Bologan at the Dresdner
Porzellan Cup 1997, transposing to
<u>A4) 7.♗e3</u>. Did Shirov sense an
improvement over the model game
below? If so, I haven't found it. After the text Burovic–Monange,
Torcy 1991 continued **8.♘g3 ♘c2**
9.♔f2 ♗g6 10.♗e3 ♗c5!
10...♘a1 11.ef7 ♔f7 12.♗d3 =.
11.♘a3 ♘e3 12.♔e3 ♘g4! By
spurning the offer of material, Black
scores a surprise mating attack.
13.fg4 ♛g5

(see next diagram)

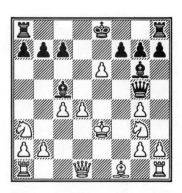

14.♔f3 14.♔e2 ♛g4 15.♔e1
♗b4 16.♔f2 ♛f4 17.♔e2 0-0! −+;
14.♔f2 ♛f4 15.♛f3 ♛d4 16.♔e1
♗b4 17.♔e2 ♛b2 −+. **14...fe6**
15.♗d3 0-0 16.♘f5 16.♔e2
♛g4 17.♔d2 ♛d4 −+. **16...ef5**
17.dc5 fg4 18.♔g3 Or 18.♔e2
♖ae8 19.♗e4 ♖e4 20.♔d3 ♛e3
21.♔c2 ♖c4#. **18...h5 19.h3 h4**
20.♔h2 g3 21.♔g1 ♛e3#, 0-1.
A showcase for Black's attacking
possibilities.

A3) 7.d5? ♘b4! A simultaneous
game Topalov–Schmitt, Frankfurt
1997 went 7...♗b4 8.♘c3 ♛e7
9.dc6 ♗e6 10.♗e3 0-0 11.♔f2
♖fe8 12.♘e4 13.fe4 ♛h4 14.g3
♛e4 15.♗g2 ♛e5 16.♘f3 ♛b2
17.♛e2 ♛a3 18.♖hd1 ♗c4
19.♛c4 ♛e3 20.♔f1 ♗c5 21.♛c2
b6 22.♖e1 ♛h6 23.♛f5 ♖e6
24.♖e6 fe6 25.♛g5 ♛g5 26.♘g5
♖f8 27.♘f3 g5 28.h3 h5 29.g4 hg4
30.hg4 ♖f4, 1/2-1/2. One is left
with the distinct impression that

Black got away with some very unsound razzle-dazzle! After 7...♘b4!, Black has distinctly better prospects:

A31) 8.♕a4 b5! 9.♕b5 c6 10.ef7 (10.dc6?? ♘c2 11.♔f2 ♕d4 12.♔e2 ♗d3) **10...♔f7 11.♕b7 ♗e7 12.♘a3 ♖e8 13.♗e3 ♖b8 14.♕a7 ♖a8 15.♕b7 ♖a3 16.ba3 ♘c2 17.♔f2 ♘a1 18.g4 ♗g4!** with a strong attack to follow.

A32) 8.♘a3 ♗c5 9.♕a4 9.g4 ♘g4!. **9...c6 10.♗e3** 10.♗d2 ♕d6, △ 11...♕e5. **10...♕e7**, and White can "consolidate" his two pawn lead with **11.dc6 bc6 12.♗c5 ♕c5 13.ef7 ♔f7** – only trouble is, now he's busted!

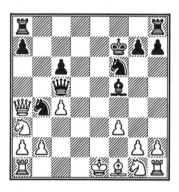

A word like "compensation" cannot do justice to such a lopsided position!

A4) 7.♗e3 The most important continuation. White attempts to complete a harmonious development while "fortressing" on the e-file. Frequently Black has opportunities for a very promising Exchange sacrifice on e3.

Now Black must choose between:

→ **A41) 7...♕e7**
→ **A42) 7...♘b4!?**
→ **A43) 7...fe6!?**
→ **A44) 7...♗b4**

A41) 7...♕e7 This move speeds up Queenside castling, but it looks a tad awkward obstructing his dark-squared Bishop's development. Still, Black plans to strike with ...♕b4 attacking weak pawns at b2 and c4, nor should White attempt 8.a3?! 0-0-0 9.♕d2 ♘d4 10.♗d4 ♕e6 11.♘e2 c5 12.♕e3 cd4 13.♕e6 ♗e6 ∓ as in Borge–Martin, Iceland 1995. We therefore consider three responses:

→ **A411) 8.♗d3**
→ **A412) 8.♘c3**
→ **A413) 8.ef7!**

A411) 8.♗d3 ♕e6 9.♗f5 ♕e3 10.♕e2 ♕e2 11.♘e2 g6! 12.♗c2 0-0-0 =∞ (Sariego). His point is that after **13.d5 ♘b4 14.♘a3 ♗c5**, △ 15...♖e8, White must return a pawn to complete his development.

A412) 8.♘c3 0-0-0! 9.♔f2 If 9.♕d2 ♘b4! 10.0-0-0 ♕e6 11.g4!? (11.d5 ♘a2! 12.♘a2 ♕a6 =; 11.a3? ♘c2 12.♘e4 [12.♗f2?? ♘a1! −+] 12...♘e4 ∓) 11...♘g4! 12.fg4 ♗e4 13.♗g5! ♗h1 14.♗d8 ♔d8 15.h3 ♗e7 =. **9...♕b4! 10.♘ge2** Not 10.ef7? ♘d4 11.♗d4 ♖d4 12.♕d4 ♗c5 −+.

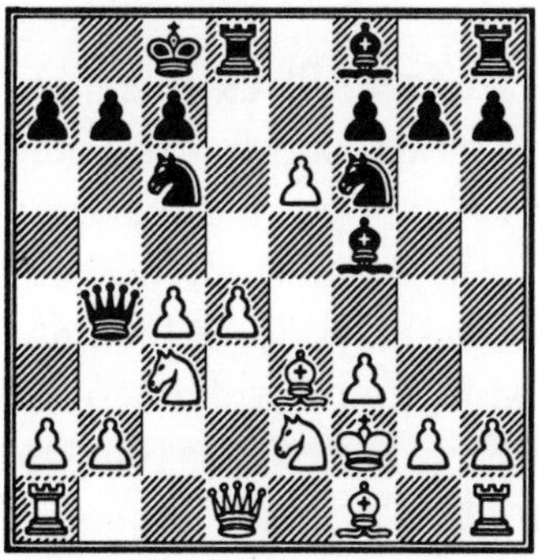

If now 10...fe6 11.♕b3 ±, and if 10...♕b2 11.ef7!? (11.g4 ♗e6 =) 11...♘e5 12.de5 ♖d1 13.♖d1 ♘d7 14.♖d2 ±. Otherwise we examine:

→ **A4121) 10...♗e6**
→ **A4122) 10...♕c4!**

A4121) 10...♗e6 11.b3 ♕a5 11...♘d4 12.a3 ♕a5 13.b4 ♘e2 14.ba5 ♖d1 15.♘d1! +−. **12.a3 ♘e7 13.♗d2 ♘f5 14.b4** 14.♘d5 ♕a6 15.♘f6 gf6 16.♗c3 ♕b6!. **14...♕b6 15.c5 ♕c6 16.b5 ♕e8 17.♕a4 ♗c5 18.dc5 ♖d2 19.♕a7 ♗c4 20.c6 bc6 21.♕a8 ♔d7 22.♕c6 ♔c8 23.♕c4** 23.♕a8 = Mainka–Sariego, Bayamo 1995. **23...♕e3 24.♔e1 ♖hd8** 24...♘d4? 25.♘d1! +−. **25.♕f4! ♕f4 26.♘f4 ♘e3 27.♖c1 ♘c2 28.♖c2 ♖c2 29.♘fe2 ♖d3 30.a4! ♖cc3 31.♘c3 ♖c3 32.a5** ± (at least!).

A4122) 10...♕c4! 11.♘g3 11.d5 ♕h4 12.g3 ♕b4 13.♕b3 ♗c5! ∓; 11.♘f4 ♕b4 ∓. **11...♕e6 12.d5 ♘d5 13.♘d5 ♕d5** 13...♖d5 14.♗c4 ±. **14.♕d5 ♖d5 15.♗c4 ♖e5 16.f4** 16.♗f7 =. **16...♖e3! ♖e3 17.♔e3 ♗c5 18.♔e2 ♗g4 19.♔f1 ♖d8** =∞.

A413) 8.ef7! ♕f7 9.♘c3! Better than 9.♗d3 (Andreev–Kazakov, Russian Ch. 1996) 9...♕g6! 10.♗f5

♕g2 11.d5 ♘e7 ∓ (or ∞!). **9...0-0-0 10.♗d3 ♗d3** 10...♗g6 11.♘ge2 ♗c5 12.♕d2 ♖he8 13.0-0 ±. **11.♕d3 ♔b8!?** △ 12...♘e5. **12.d5** 12.b3 ♘b4 13.♕d2 ♕g6 14.0-0-0 ♘bd5! 15.♔b2 ♘c3 16.♔c3 ♗a3 ⩲. **12...♘b4 13.♕d2 ♕g6 14.0-0-0 ♘fd5!? 15.cd5 ♖d5 16.♕f2 ♖d1 17.♔d1 ♗e7 18.♕e2! ♖d8 19.♔e1** ±. Black needs to find improvements here if 7...♕e7 hopes to be viable.

A42) 7...♘b4!? Relatively untested, this try deserves to be considered on its merits rather than the result of one game, which Black lost. **8.♘a3** If 8.ef7 ♔f7 9.♘a3 ♗d6 10.♔f2 ♖e8 11.♕d2 ♕d7, △ 12...♖e7 and 13...♖ae8 ⩲. It is not easy to find an acceptable approach to developing White's Kingside. **8...fe6 9.g4** White's normal scheme of development with ♘e2 or ♗d3 has been precluded by Black's seventh move. Still, one gasps to see such a move as this! **9...♗g6 10.♘h3 ♗d6 11.♕a4 c6 12.♕b3!** Not 12.c5? ♘bd5.

(see next diagram)

12...a5! An improvement over 12...♕a5? 13.♗d2 c5 14.♘b5 0-0-0 15.a3 ♗b8 16.♖c1 winning the pinned Knight in Kovalev-

After 12.♕b3!

Meyer, 1996. After the text, the aggressive **13.c5!? ♗e7 14.♕e6? ♗f7** puts White's Queen in an embarrassing spot: **15.♕e5 0-0 16.♘g5 ♘d7 17.♕f5 ♗g6 18.♕e6 ♔h8 19.h4 ♘d5 20.h5 ♗e8 21.f4 ♗g5 22.fg5 ♗f7** −+. If White doesn't respond with 13.c5, he will still have a long-term weakness at f3. This factor, along with Black's better piece placement, should be ample compensation for the gambit pawn.

A43) 7...fe6!? Black cuts his losses to one pawn, and forces White to defend his d4 pawn directly as it is now restrained from advancing. Although Black loses his immediate e-file counterplay, that may come about later with a timely ...e5. **8.♘c3 ♕d7**

(see next diagram)

1.e4 d5 2.ed5 ♘f6 3.d4 ♗g4

There may now follow from the diagram:

→ **A431) 9.♘ge2?**
→ **A432) 9.g4?!**
→ **A433) 9.a3**

A431) 9.♘ge2? ♘b4! is awkward for White: **10.♔f2 ♘c2 11.♖c1 ♘e3 12.♔e3 e5!** with strong counterplay based on wresting control of the diagonal a7-g1. Fantasy line: **13.♕a4 ed4 14.♘d4 c6 15.♕a5!? ♗g6 16.♖d1 ♗d6 17.♔f2 0-0 18.♔g1 b6 19.♕a4 ♗c5 20.♘e2 ♖ae8 21.b4 ♖e2 22.bc5 ♗c2! −+ 23.♘e2 ♗d1 24.♕b4 ♗e2 25.♗e2 ♕d4 26.♔f1 ♘e4 27.♔e1 ♕f2 28.♔d1 ♖d8 29.♔c1 ♕e3 30.♔b1 ♘c3 31.♔a1** 31.♔c2 ♖d2. **31...♖d2 −+.**

A432) 9.g4?! This move is clearly anti-positional now that the f-file is half open, but it does offer a way to pressure e6 by using the h3-c8 diagonal. Black must be ready to change plans. **9...♗g6 10.g5 ♘h5 11.♗h3** The threat of d4-d5 means Black must forget about castling Queenside. However, he simply turns his focus to the weakened f-file and prepares ...0-0. **11...♕f7 12.a3** On 12.♕b3 best is 12...♘b4! 13.♘e4 ♘f4 14.♗f1 ♗e4 15.fe4 ♕g6! ∓. **12...♘f4 13.♘e4 ♖d8 14.♗f1** Otherwise it is hard for White to complete his development. **14...♗e7 15.♘h3 ♘h3 16.♗h3 0-0 17.0-0 ♘d4!** ∓ After **18.♗d4 e5**, Black equalizes the material with a superior position, based on his Bishop pair and White's weakened Kingside.

A433) 9.a3 A useful move for attack and defense. **9...0-0-0 10.♘ge2 ♕e8!**

Black sets about his counterplay based on ...e5. A pointless waste of tempo is 10...♕f7?! 11.♕b3 ♕e8 as played in Nikolenko–Saulin, Russia 1996. 10...g5!? with the idea of positioning the Queen at g7 was tried in Bologan–Shirov, Dresden Cup 1997 – although I am doubtful of Black's compensation after 11.♗g5. The game continued instead 11.♕a4 ♕g7 12.0-0-0 ♘d7 13.b4 ♘b6 14.♕b3 ♗e7 15.d5 ed5 16.cd5 ♕e5! 17.♗f2! (17.♗b6 ab6 18.dc6 ♕e3 19.♔b2 ♖d2! 20.♖d2 ♕d2 21.♔a1 ♗f6 and Black's attack is well worth the sacrificed piece) 17...♗f6 18.dc6 ♗e6 19.cb7 ♔b7 20.♕c2 ♗f5 21.♕b3 ♗e6 22.♕b1 ♖d1 23.♘d1 ♗f5 24.♕b2 ♕d6 25.♗d4 ♖d8 26.♘e3 ♗d4 27.♕d4 ♕e6 28.♕d8 ♕e3 29.♕d2 ♕a3 30.♔d1 ♗d3 31.♘c1 ♘c4 and now instead of 32.♕d3? ♘b2 =, White is winning with 32.♕g5 +−.

From the diagram (after 10...♕e8!) White plays **11.♕a4**, planning to castle long. We consider two responses:

A4331) 11...♘d7 With the idea of 12.0-0-0? ♘b6 13.♕b3 ♘a5 and 14...♘ac4. **12.c5** Better is 12.♘e4! ♘b6 13.♕c2 intending 14.♖d1 and ♘2g3 ±. The text led to extreme complications resolving into an equal endgame in Batsanin–Saulin, Russia 1996: **12...e5 13.d5**

♘d4 14.c6 ♘c5 15.♕a7 ♘d3 16.♔d1 ♘b2 17.♔c1 ♘d3 18.♔b1 ♘c6 19.dc6 ♕c6 20.♕a8 ♔d7 21.♕a5 ♕e6 22.♘c1 ♘f2 23.♔b2 ♘h1 24.♘b3 b6 25.♖d1 ♗d6 26.♕b5 c6 27.♕b6 ♖b8 28.♘c5 ♔e7 29.♘e6 ♗e6 30.♕b8 ♖b8 Now instead of 31.♔c2? ♗b3 ∓, White should have equalized with **31.♗b5!**.

A4332) 11...e5! 12.d5 ♘d4

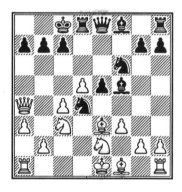

The Center Counter has many examples of Queens-off middlegames where Black has good compensation for a pawn deficit – and this is one of them. **13.♕e8** Capturing at d4 would lose a piece. **13...♘c2** Equally good is 13...♖e8, since White has nothing better than to transpose with 14.♔f2 or 14.♖c1. **14.♔f2 ♖e8 15.♖c1 ♘e3 16.♔e3 e4!** Stronger than 16...♗c5 17.♔d2 e4 18.♘g3!. **17.f4** Not 17.♘g3?? ef3 18.♔f3 ♗g4 which leads to mate, or

17.b4 ef3 18.♔f3 ♘g4 19.♘g3 (19.♘d4 ♗d7) 19...♖e3 20.♔f4 ♗d6! 21.♔f5 (21.♔g5 ♗d7 −+) 21...♘f2 −+ with a mating net. **17...♘g4 18.♔d2** Or 18.♔d4? c5 19.dc6 ♖d8 20.♘d5 bc6 21.♘g3 g6 ∓. **18...e3 19.♔e1 ♘f2 20.♘d4 ♘h1 21.♘f5 ♘f2** ∓ White does not have enough for the Exchange.

A44) 7...♗b4 This natural developing move has been the main line.

White can interpose with either:

→ **A441) 8.♘c3**
→ **A442) 8.♘d2!**

A441) 8.♘c3 ♕e7 9.♗d3 9.d5? lost quickly in Wang–Damaso (China-Portugal Match), Macao 1996 after 9...0-0-0 10.♕a4 ♘d5! 11.cd5 ♕h4 12.♔d1?? (12.g3?? ♗c3 and 13...♕a4; 12.♔e2 ♘d4 13.♗d4 [13.♔d2 ♗c3 14.♔c3 ♘e2 15.♔b3 ♗c2 −+] 13...♕d4 14.♕b3 ♗c5 15.♘h3 ♖he8 16.♔e1 ♗h3 17.gh3 ♕f2 18.♔d1 ♕f3 −+) 12...♖d5 13.♘d5 (13.♔e2 ♗d3 −+) 13...♕e1#, 0-1. **9...♗e6 10.♔f2** If 10.♕e2?! 0-0-0 11.a3 (Almasi–Adorjan, Zalakaros 1992) 11...♘d4! 12.♗d4 ♖d4 13.ab4 ♖d3 14.♖a7 ♔b8 15.♖a4 ♖e8 16.b5 ♗c4! and Black is winning. **10...0-0-0 11.♘ge2 ♖he8 12.♕d2!?** Probably best here is 12.♕c1(!) ♗c5 13.♖e1 (13.♖d1 ♘d4 14.♘d4 ♗d4 15.♗d4 ♖d4 16.♘b5 ♖h4!) 13...♘d4 14.♘d4 ♗d4 15.♗d4 ♖d4 16.♕e3 ♖ed8 17.♖ad1 ♕d7 18.♗c2 c6, 1/2-1/2 was deFirmian–Vescovi, Bermuda Triangle 1996. **12...g5!**

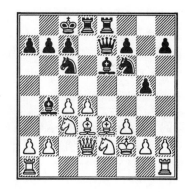

In Boulard–Eliet (French Team Championship 1993) Black delayed this for a move: 12...♔b8 13.♖he1 g5 14.a3 (14.♗g5 ♘d4 15.♕f4 ♕c5!! 16.♔f1 ♘f3! 17.♕f3 ♕g5 ∓) 14...♗c3 15.♕c3 g4 16.♘f4 gf3 17.gf3 ♘g4! 18.fg4 ♕h4, and now instead of 19.♔e2?

White is winning with 19.♔g1! ♕g4 (19...♗g4 20.♗f2 or 20.♘g2) 20.♘g2! +–. Even after 19.♔e2? ♗g4 20.♔d2 ♕h2, White could have forced Black to take a perpetual with 21.♘e2 ♖e3 22.♔e3 ♕h6 23.♔f2 ♕h2 =.

The tempo saved by the 12...g5! text move is not trivial. Black has excellent winning chances from the last diagram, as these examples show:

→ **A4411) 13.a3**
→ **A4412) 13.♗g5**
→ **A4413) 13.d5**

A4411) 13.a3 ♗c3 14.♕c3 g4 15.♖he1 gf3 16.gf3 ♘h5 17.♗h7 ♗c4! Even stronger than 17...♕h4 right away. Black is winning.

A4412) 13.♗g5 ♘d4 14.♕f4 Or 14.♘d4 ♖d4 15.♗e3 ♖dd8 16.♕e2 ♗c5 with strong pressure, e.g. 17.♘d1 ♘h5 18.g3 ♗h3 19.♗c5 ♕c5 20.♘e3 f5 ∓. **14...♕c5 15.♔f1 ♘e2 16.♗e2 ♗c3 17.bc3 ♘h5** with more than enough compensation for the pawn: **18.♕e3** Also 18.♕h4 f6. **18...♕e3 19.♗e3 ♗c4 20.♗c4 ♖e3 21.♗f7 ♘f4 ∓**.

A4413) 13.d5 ♘e5 14.♗g5 ♘d3 15.♕d3 ♘g4 16.fg4 ♕g5 17.h3 ♗c5 18.♔e1 18.♔f1 f5 19.♘a4 ♗e3 20.h4 ♕g4! 21.♕e3 ♗d5 22.♕f2 ♖e2 –+. **18...f5 19.♖f1 c6!** 19...fg4 20.♕h7 gh3 21.gh3 ♕e3 22.♕e4! ±. **20.gf5 ♗f7**

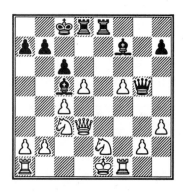

21.g4 ♖e3 22.♕d2 cd5! 22...♕h4 23.♔d1 ♕h3 24.♔c2 cd5 25.♘f4 ♕g4 26.cd5 ♕f5 27.♘d3 ♕d3 (27...♕g6 28.♖f7 ±) 28.♕d3 ♗g6 29.♖ad1 ♖d3 30.♖d3 ♗d4 =. **23.cd5 ♕h4 24.♔d1 ♕h3 25.♔c2 ♗d5! 26.♘f4 ♗e4 27.♘e4 ♖d2 28.♔d2 ♗b4 29.♘c3 ♕g3 ∓**.

A442) 8.♘d2! White sets up a future a2-a3, when his Queen can recapture. Note that the d-pawn is off limits: 8...♘d4?? 9.♗d4 ♕d4 10.♕a4 △ 11.♕b4 winning a piece. Because of the text move, there has been a trend away from 7...♗b4 to alternatives such as <u>A41) 7...♕e7</u>.

1.e4 d5 2.ed5 ♘f6 3.d4 ♗g4

I believe Black has not yet put 8.♘d2 to its most serious test. We now examine the Black choices:

→ **A4421) 8...♕e7(?)**
→ **A4422) 8...0-0!?**

A4421) 8...♕e7(?) This plan is the normal procedure, preparing ...0-0-0. But in practice White has been able to shake off the pressure and consolidate his extra pawn, suggesting to me that the text is too slow. **9.a3!** On 9.d5?! 0-0-0! is a thematic piece sac:

10.dc6 ♕e6 11.cb7 ♔b8 12.♕e2 ♖he8 13.♔f2 (13.0-0-0 ♕e3 14.♕e3 ♖e3, △ 15...♖c3!! −+) 13...♖d2! 14.♗d2 ♗c5 15.♔e1 ♕b6! ∓. If White declines the piece with 10.a3 ♗d2 11.♗d2 ♘d4, he is still subject to a brisk attack. **9...♕e6 10.♔f2 ♗d2 11.♕d2 0-0-0 12.♕c3 ♕d6** This looks like a place to search for improvements, but nothing seems to work:

1) **12...♖he8 13.d5 ♖d5 14.cd5 ♘d5 15.♗c4! ♕e3 16.♕e3 ♘e3 17.♖e1 +−**.

2) **12...♗g6!? 13.♘e2! ±**, but not 13.d5? ♕f5 14.♔e1 ♘e5 15.♔d2 ♖he8 16.♖e1 ♘c4! 17.♗c4 ♘d5 −+. After 13.♘e2 there followed **13...♖he8 14.♖d1 h6 15.♘g3 ♗h7 16.♗e2 g5 17.♖he1 ♖g8 18.d5 ♕e7 19.c5 ♘e5 20.d6 ±** with an extra pawn and the attack for White in Pina–A.Carvalho, World Junior Ch. 1996.

A4422) 8...0-0!?

This is my suggestion to resurrect Black's chances in the A442) 8.♘d2 line. We will look at the following:

→ **A44221) 9.a3**
→ **A44222) 9.d5**

A44221) 9.a3 Plausible, but Black has **9...♘d4!**, a very dangerous piece sacrifice that keeps White's King pinned down in the center. Two possibilities:

1) 10.♗d4 ♛d4 11.ab4 ♛b2, and now:

1a) 12.ef7 ♖f7 13.♛a4 ♛e5 13...♖e7 14.♘e2 ♗d3 15.♛a3 ±. **14.♘e2 ♗d3 15.♖a3 ♖d8 16.♛a7 ♖e7 17.♛c5 ♛e6 18.♛f2 ♛e5 19.♖a2 ♛c3 20.♔d1 ♗e2 21.♗e2 ♖e3! −+** (△ 22...♛b3).

1b) 12.b5 ♖ae8!? 13.♛c1 Not 13.♖a7? ♖a8! −+. **13...♖e6 14.♘e2 ♛e5 15.♘b3!** Again mistaken would be 15.♖a7? ♗d3 16.♛a1 ♛g5! 17.f4 ♛g4 18.h3 ♛g3 19.♔d1 ♛f2 ∓. **15...♗d3 16.f4 ♛d6 17.♛a3** Black is also better after 17.c5 ♛d5 18.♛d1 ♘g4! 19.♖a4! ♘e3 20.♖d4 ♗e2 21.♖d5 ♗d1 22.♖d1 ♘d1 23.♔d1 ♖d8 24.♔c2 ♖e1 ∓. **17...♛f4 18.♘c5 ♖e2 19.♗e2 ♗e2 20.♔e2 ♖e8 21.♔d1 ♘g4! 22.♔c2 ♛c4 23.♔b1 ♛b5 24.♔c1** 24.♘b3 ♖e3 −+. **24...♘f2 25.♖g1 ♛c5! ∓.**

2) 10.ab4 White takes half a loaf – two minors for the Rook – but he's

not yet off the hook, as **10...♘c2 11.♔f2 ♖e8!** is still dangerous.

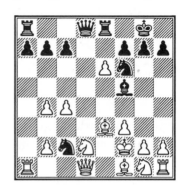

Best play may level out:

2a) 12.♖c1? ♘e3 13.♔e3 ♖e6 14.♘e4 ♛e7 15.♗d3 ♖d8 16.♛c2 ♘e4 17.fe4 17.♗e4 ♗e4 18.fe4 ♛g5 −+. **17...♖d3 18.♛d3 ♗e4 19.♛c3 ♛g5 −+.**

2b) 12.ef7? ♔f7 13.♖a3 ♘e3 14.♖e3 ♛d4 15.♛e2 ♛f4 16.g3 ♘g4 17.♔e1 ♛e3 18.fg4 ♛d4 19.gf5 ♖e2 20.♘e2 ♛b2 ∓.

2c) 12.♖a3 ♖e6 13.♗e2 Or 13.♘e2 ♘a3 14.♘d4 ♘c4 15.♗c4 ♖e5 ∞. **13...♘e3 14.♖e3 ♖e3 15.♔e3 ♛e7 16.♔f2 ♖d8 17.c5 ♛d7! 18.♔e1 ♛d4 19.♛c1 ♘d5 20.g4 ♗g6 21.♘h3 ♖e8 22.♘f2 ♛b4** 22...♖e2 23.♔e2 ♘f4 24.♔d1! ♛f2 25.♛c4 ♘d3 26.♛c3 ♛g2

27.♖f1 ♕h2 28.♕d4 ♕h4 29.♘e4 ±. 23.♘fe4 ♗e4 24.fe4 ♖e4 25.♕c2 ♖e2 26.♔e2 ♕g4 with perpetual check.

A44222) 9.d5 White now gains the advantage after a "normal" reply like 9...♘e5. But this is not a normal position! With White's King in the center and the ♗e3 on shaky ground, Black should try **9...♖e8!**

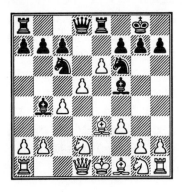

Some grisly possibilities:

1) **10.dc6 ♖e6 11.♔f2** 11.♕e2 ♕e7 12.♔f2 ♖e3!. **11...♖e3! 12.♔e3 ♗c5 13.♔e2** 13.♔f4 ♕d6 14.♔f5 ♗e3! and mate next move. **13...♕e7 14.♘e4 ♘e4 15.fe4 ♕e4 16.♔d2 ♕e3#.**

2) **10.g4 ♗e6! 11.dc6 ♗d5! 12.cd5 ♘d5 −+** with threats of 13...♕h4 14.♔e2 ♘f4#, or 13...♘e3 etc.

3) **10.♔f2 ♘e5** Now that a check on g4 is possible, this move is strong. **11.g4 ♘fg4 12.fg4 ♘g4 13.♔e2 ♖e6! 14.de6 ♕d3 −+.**

4) **10.♘e2 ♘e5 11.♘d4 fe6 12.a3 ♗f8 13.de6** Worse is 13.g4? ♘fg4 14.fg4 ♘g4 15.♗f4 ed5 16.♗e2 ♘f2! 17.♔f2 ♕h4 18.♔g1 (18.♔g2 ♗h3) ♕f4 19.♘2f3 ♗c5 20.♔g2 ♗d4 21.♘d4 ♖e2! −+. **13...♗g6 14.♕b3 c5 15.♘c2 ♖e6 16.0-0-0 ♕e7 17.♗e2** Or 17.♘b1 =. **17...♖d8 18.♗g5** 18.♖he1 ♘d3 ∓. **18...♘f7 19.♗f6 gf6 ∓.**

To sum up, we recommend that Black respond to 8.♘d2 with 8...0-0!, throwing pawns (or even pieces) to the wind. White's lagging development and exposed King position offer plenty of justification for this "scorched earth" policy.

B) 5.♗b5

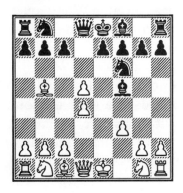

This is probably more correct than 5.c4, and certainly safer as it allows White rapid development and Kingside castling. After seeing some cases above in which White was desperate to get his Kingside off the back row, castling must seem luxurious indeed! The main line is **5...♘bd7**, but in passing we also consider:

1) **5...♗d7 6.♗c4 b5** Black cuts off support to the d5 pawn. This resembles the line 3.♗b5 ♗d7 4.♗c4 b5!? except that White has gotten in two free moves – the useful d4 and the doubtful f3. **7.♗b3 g6 8.♘e2 ♗g7 9.c3 0-0 10.0-0 ♗f5 11.♘f4 ♘bd7 12.♘a3 b4 13.♘c2 bc3 14.bc3 ♗c2 15.♕c2 ♘b6** Black regains his pawn at the cost of the Bishop pair. Now a mistake would be 16.c4? ♘fd5 17.♘d5 ♘d5 18.cd5 ♗d4 ∓, but one game went **16.h4 a5 17.a4 ♘fd5 18.♖d1 ±** and after long maneuvering White squeezed out a win (Kazmin–Emeljanov, 1996).

2) **5...c6!? 6.dc6 ♕a5 7.♘c3 ♘c6** leads to a great firestorm of complications. We examine two options for White in the following position:

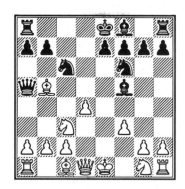

2a) **8.♘ge2 0-0-0 9.♗c6 bc6 10.♗d2 e5 11.♘e4 ♕b6 12.♘4g3 ♗g6 13.de5 ♘d5 14.♕c1 ♗c5 15.♘e4 ♗e4 16.fe4 ♘e3 17.♘f4 ♘g4 18.♘d3 ♗g1 19.♔e2 ♖d3 20.♕g1 ♖d4 21.♗c3 ♕b5 22.♔e1 ♖e4 23.♔d2 ♕e2 24.♔c1 ♘e3 25.♕e3 ♖e3 26.a3 ♖d8, 0-1** was Mezouachi–Mevel, Metz 1994.

2b) **8.♗d2 0-0-0 9.a4 ♕c7 10.♗c6 bc6 11.f4 ♖d4 12.♘f3 ♖d8 13.♘e5 e6 14.♕e2 ♔b7 15.g4 ♗g6 16.h4 ♗b4 17.0-0-0 ♖d4 18.h5 ♗e4 19.♘e4 ♖e4 20.♕f3 ♕a5 21.c3 ♗c5 22.g5 ♕a4 23.gf6 gf6 24.♘d3 ♗b6 25.f5 ♖d8 26.♔b1 ♖d5 27.♘b4 ♖de5 28.♗f4 ef5 29.♗e5 fe5 30.♕f5 ♖f4 31.♕d7 ♗c7 32.♕d3 a5 33.♕c2 ♕b5 34.♘d3 ♖e4 35.♘c5 ♕c5 36.♕e4 a4 37.♕a4 e4 38.♕e4 f5 39.♕f3**

f4 40.♖hf1 ♛f5 41.♛d3 ♛h5 42.♛e4 f3 43.♛f3 ♛g6 44.♛f5, 1-0. Pedersen–Rewitz, Denmark 1996.

After **5.♗b5 ♘bd7** we consider the following moves:

→ **B1) 6.♘c3**

→ **B2) 6.c4**

B1) 6.♘c3

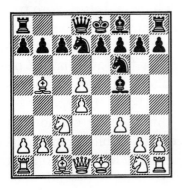

Rarely played, this move has more than a drop of poison. Black regains the pawn, but he risks having a weakened position along with lagging development and a space disadvantage. **6...a6 7.♗a4** Insipid is 7.♗d3 ♗d3 8.♛d3 ♘b6 9.♘ge2 ♘fd5!? (9...♘bd5 =) 10.♘e4 e6 11.0-0 ♘b4 12.♛d1 ♗e7 13.c3 ♘c6 14.♗e3 0-0 15.♔f2 a5 = as in A.Nikitin–Ulko, Moscow 1994. **7...b5 8.♗b3 ♘b6 9.♘ge2 ♘bd5** Instead, 9...g6!? leads to unclear play similar to some of the

3.♗b5 lines. One game continued 10.♘f4 ♗g7 11.g4 b4 12.♘a4 ♘a4 13.♗a4 ♗d7 14.♗b3 ♗c8 15.♗d2 ♛d6 16.♛e2 0-0 17.g5 ♘d7 18.♛c4 a5 19.♛c6, and now not 19...♛c6 as in Prie–Patrat, Paris 1990 but rather 19...♘b6! (△ 20...a4) 20.c3 bc3 21.bc3 e5! with excellent compensation for the pawn, e.g. 22.♛d6 cd6 23.de5 ♗e5 ⯹, or 22.de5 ♛e5 23.♔f2 ♗d7 24.♛c5 ♖fe8 25.♖hg1 ♗f8 26.♛e3 ♛d6 27.♛d3 ♗f5 28.♛f1 a4 29.♗d1 ♘d5 –+. **10.♘d5 ♘d5 11.♘g3**

Black must attend to his threatened Bishop:

→ **B11) 11...♗g6**

→ **B12) 11...g6**

B11) 11...♗g6?! A natural response, but Black tends to get overrun by a strong White initiative based on f4-f5. **12.c4** Alternatively, 12.f4 e6 13.f5 ef5 14.0-0 f4

15.♘h5 c5 16.♖e1 ♝e7 17.dc5
♘e3 18.♕d8 ♚d8 19.♘f4 ♘c4
20.♝c4 bc4 21.♝e3 ♝c2 22.♖ac1
♝a4 23.♘d5 ♝b5 24.♖cd1 ♖c8,
1-0 was K.Georgiev–Jadoul, Belfort
1989. **12...♘b6 13.c5 ♘d5 14.0-0
e6 15.f4 f5** A horrible move to
have to make! **16.♕e2 ♕d7
17.a4 ♖b8 18.ab5 ab5 19.♖a7
♝e7 20.♝d5 ♕d5 21.♖c7 h5
22.♕e5 ♕e5 23.fe5 h4 24.♘e2
h3 25.gh3, 1-0.** Duggan–Pullinger,
St. Heliers (Jersey) 1997.

B12) 11...g6!

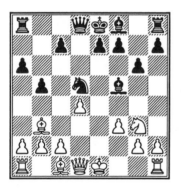

A suggestion of NM Sid Pickard.
Black develops his King's Bishop on
the long diagonal, saving time and
avoiding the problems with White's
f-pawn thrust seen in the previous
examples. Although this line needs
testing, White appears to get no
more than equality from the opening. Play might continue **12.♘f5
gf5 13.c4** 13.c3!?. **13...♘b6 14.c5
♘d5 15.a4 e6 16.ab5 ab5**

17.♖a8 ♕a8 18.0-0 18.♕d3
♕a5 19.♕d2 ♕a8. **18...♝g7
19.♕d3 0-0 20.♖d1 ♕c6 =.**

B2) 6.c4 By far the most popular
move, which tempers rapid development with greed. We consider:

→ **B21) 6...a6**
→ **B22) 6...e6**

There has long been a debate over
which move is better. With 6...a6,
White must either help Black's
Queenside development with
7.♝d7 or face a disruptive pawn
lever after 7.♝a4 b5. I believe the
latter evil has been overvalued – for
one thing, Black cannot castle
Queenside. White seems able to
consolidate his pawn once the
smoke clears. The older move
6...e6 creates counterplay much as
in the Icelandic Gambit (1.e4 d5
2.ed5 ♘f6 3.c4 e6 4.de6 ♝e6). It
is the sturdier of the two choices,
and has withstood persistent attempts at refutation.

B21) 6...a6

White's play can be divided as
follows:

→ **B211) 7.♝d7**
→ **B212) 7.♝a4**

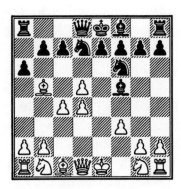

After 6...a6

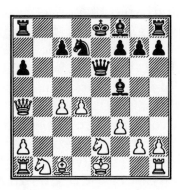

Two examples from the diagram:

B211) 7.♗d7 ♕d7 8.♘e2 Another way is 8.♘c3 e6! 9.de6 (9.♗g5!? ♗b4) 9...♕e6 10.♕e2 ♗b4 11.♗d2 0-0-0 12.♕e6 ♗e6 13.d5 ♗f5 14.a3 ♖he8 15.♔d1 ♗c5 16.♘ge2 c6! as in Susterman–Carvallo (World Cadet Ch.), Duisburg 1992. Now there might have followed 17.b4 ♗a7 18.dc6 ♗e3 19.cb7 ♔b7 20.♖a2 ♗e6! ⩱. After the text Black has:

➡ **B2111) 8...b5!?**
➡ **B2112) 8...e6**

B2111) 8...b5!? This move reduces the White pawn chain to create an additional object of attack at c4. **9.b3 bc4 10.bc4 e6 11.de6 ♕e6 12.♕a4** Or 12.d5 ♕e5 13.♕d4 ♕d4 14.♘d4 ♗d3 15.♘d2 ♗b4 ⩱. **12...♘d7**

(see next diagram)

1) **13.♘c3 ♗d3 14.c5** 14.d5 ♕f6 15.♕c6 ♕c6 16.dc6 ♘e5 17.♗f4 ♘c6 18.♗c7 ♗c4 =, or even ⩱. **14...♗e7 15.♗f4 0-0 16.0-0 ♘c5 17.♕d1** 17.dc5 ♗c5 18.♔h1 ♗e2 19.♖fe1 ♕c4 (19...♗b5!? 20.♘b5 ab5 21.♕b5 ♕b6 22.♕d7 ♗d6 =) 20.♖e2 ♕c3 21.♖c1 ♕d4 22.♕d4 ♗d4 23.♖c7 ♖fe8 =. **17...♕c4! 18.dc5 ♗c5 19.♔h1 ♖fe8** (Stepovoj–Ulko, Moscow Ch. 1996) and White can save the day with **20.♖e1 ♗f2 21.♕b3 ♖e2 22.♘e2 ♕b3 23.ab3 ♗e1 24.♖e1 ♖e8 25.♗c7 =.** The actual game ended abruptly after 20.♖c1? ♗a3 21.♖e1?? (21.♖f2 ♗e2 22.♘e2 ♗c1 23.♕c1 ♕a2 ⩱) 21...♗c1 22.♘c1 ♗c2, 0-1.

2) **13.♔f2! ♗d3** Quite inferior is 13...♗d6?! 14.c5 ♗b1 15.♖b1 ♗e7 16.♗e3 g5 17.d5! ♕d5

18.♖hd1 ♕e6 19.♘d4 +− with a crushing position in Cobb–Hebden, West Bromwich 1997. **14.♖e1 ♕c4 15.♕c4 ♗c4 16.♘f4 ♔d8** Black's King is reasonably safe in the center, but his piece coordination could be better. The following forcing continuation stifles the effectiveness of the Bishop pair. **17.♘d2! ♗b5 18.a4 ♗c6 19.d5 ♗c5 20.♔g3 ♗b7 21.♘e4 ±**.

B2112) 8...e6 9.de6 ♕e6 10.b3 10.d5?! accelerates Black's counterplay: 10...♕b6 11.♕d4 ♕d4 12.♘d4 ♗d3 13.b3 and now best is 13...b5! =. Less convincing is 13...♗c5 14.♗e3 0-0-0 15.♘c3 ♖he8 (Nicolo–Hassim Unes, IECC 1996) because of 16.♔d2! ♗g6 17.♘c2 ±. **10...0-0-0 11.0-0 ♗c5 12.♔h1 ♗d4 13.♘d4 ♕d7 14.♗b2 c5 15.b4 cd4 16.b5**

16...ab5 Instead 16...♖he8 is a recommendation of Keene and Levy, repeated by John Emms in his book. However, White has 17.ba6 ba6 18.♘a3! (Better than 18.♘d2 d3 19.♖b1 [19.c5!?] 19...♖e2 ∞ [Emms] △ 20...♗h3) 18...d3 19.c5 ♖e2 20.♗f6 gf6 21.♘c4 and Black quickly ran out of tricks in Ruben–Mongin, IECG 1996: 21...♔c7 22.♘d6 ♗h3 23.♖g1 ♖b8 24.♖b1 ♗f5 25.♖b8 ♔b8 26.♕b3 ♔a8 27.♖b1, 1-0. **17.♘a3 bc4 18.♘c4 ♔b8 19.♗a3 ♕e6!** 19...♕d5? 20.♖c1 ♖he8 21.♕d2 ♖e6 22.♘a5 with a winning attack in Lanka-Hauchard, Torcy 1991. The text not only holds on, but confers a slight advantage to Black: **20.♖c1 ♕a6 21.♗c5 ♗e6 22.♘b6 ♘d5 23.♖b1 ♗f5 24.♘d5 ♖d5 25.♖c1 ♖c8 26.♗b4 ♖c1 27.♕c1 ♕c6 28.♕d2 ♕c2 29.♕f4 ♕c7 30.♕d2 ♕c2 31.♕f4 ♕c7 32.♕d2 ♗d7 33.♖e1 ♗c6 34.♖e7 ♖d7 35.♖e8 ♖d8 36.♖e7 ♖d7 37.♖e8 ♖d8 38.♖e7, 1/2-1/2.** Palac–Liardet, Cannes 1997.

B212) 7.♗a4! This move in my opinion is the refutation of 6...a6. The Blumenfeld/Benko-style gambit with ...b5 is not to be feared, and it deprives Black of the Queenside castling option. If Black does not follow through with ...b5 it can be argued that he has only weakened a potential castling wing, and given White a tempo to get his slightly stranded b5 Bishop back in the game. To my knowledge, 7...e6 8.de6 ♗e6 has not been explored. **7...b5 8.cb5 ♘d5** 8...♘b6?! is not much of an option, e.g. 9.ba6 ♘a4 10.♕a4 ♕d7 11.♕d7 ♔d7 12.♘c3 ♖a6 13.♘ge2 e6 14.g4 ♗d3 15.de6 ♖e6 16.♔f2, and even without 16...♗b4?? 17.♘f4 Black was two pawns down for very little in Stepanov–Boudier, Cappelle la Grande 1995.

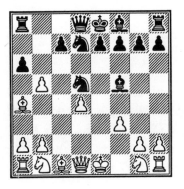

We have three examples of play from this position:

→ **B2121) 9.♘c3**
→ **B2122) 9.a3**
→ **B2123) 9.♘e2**

B2121) 9.♘c3?! Neglecting to prepare Kingside castling, White is caught off guard at d3 by the retort **9...♘b4! 10.♘e4** What else? Black has at least equality: **10...e5 11.♘e2** Worse is 11.a3 ab5 12.♗b5 ed4 13.♗f4 c6 ∓. **11...ed4 12.♘d4 ♗e4 13.fe4 ♕h4 14.g3 ♕e4 15.♕e2 ♕e2 16.♔e2 ♘c5 17.♗d1 ab5 18.♘b5 ♖a2** = Hnydiuk–Salmensuu, European Cadet Ch. 1996.

B2122) 9.a3 Playable but hardly necessary. **9...e5** Better is 9...e6 10.♘e2 ♗d6 with play as in the next line with 9.♘e2, except that here Black is effectively a tempo ahead. **10.♘e2 ♗e7 11.0-0 0-0 12.♗b3 ♘7b6 13.ba6 ♗c8 14.♘bc3 ♗a6 15.♖e1 ♘c3 16.bc3 ♗d6 17.de5** ± Acs–Conlon, Bratislava 1993.

B2123) 9.♘e2! e6 There is nothing to fear from 9...ab5 10.♗b5 ♘b4, e.g. 11.0-0! ♘c2 12.♘g3 ♘a1 (12...♗g6 13.f4 ♘a1 14.f5 ♗f5 15.♘f5 e6 17.♕f3! ±) 13.♘f5 e6 (13...g6 14.♘h6 ±) 14.♘c3 ♖a5 15.♕e2 c6 16.♗c6 ♖f5 17.♗e3 ±. **10.0-0 ♗d6 11.♘bc3 0-0** So far as in Yewdokimov–Alvarez Ibarra, San Sebastian 1993. Now White can consolidate his pawn plus with 12.♘d5 ed5 13.ba6 ♖a6 14.♗f4 ♗f4 15.♘f4

♕g5 16.♘d5 ♗h3 17.♖f2 ♗g2 18.♖g2 ♕d5 19.♗b3 ♕d6 20.♖c1 ±. The game continued along less clear lines with **12.♘g3 ♗g3 13.hg3 ♘7b6 14.♘d5 ♕d5 15.ba6 ♘a4 16.♕a4 ♗d3 17.♖d1 ♗a6 ± 18.♕b4 ♗c4 19.♗f4 ♗a2 20.♗c7 ♗b3 21.♖a8 ♖a8 22.♖c1 h6 23.♗e5 ♗a4 24.g4 ♕b3 25.♕d2 f6 26.♗f6!?**, and Black survived the attempt at violent attack to emerge with a draw.

B22) 6...e6! 7.de6 ♗e6

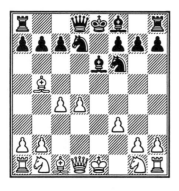

White can try one of the following moves:

→ **B221) 8.d5**
→ **B222) 8.c5**
→ **B223) 8.♘c3**

GM Vladimor Dmitrov once went into a 40-minute think against GM Kevin Spraggett (Ubeda, Spain 1996) and came up with the illogi-cal **8.♗d7?! ♕d7 9.b3**, reaching a position similar to B211) 7...♗d7 – but minus a huge tempo for White. Now best according to Spraggett is **9...♗b4! 10.♔f2** 10.♗d2 ♕d4. **10...0-0-0 11.♘e2 ♖he8** and Black has a big lead in development, as seen below.

We examine two possibilities in this sideline:

1) **12.a3 ♗c5** 12...♘g4!?. **13.♗e3 ♘g4! 14.fg4 ♗g4 15.♕c1** 15.dc5 ♕f5 −+. **15...♕f5 16.♔g3** 16.♔e1 ♕d3 −+; 16.♘f4 ♖e3! −+. **16...♗e2 17.dc5 ♖d3 −+.**

2) **12.♗d2 ♘g4! 13.fg4** 13.♔g1 ♗c4! 14.bc4 ♖e2! −+. **13...♗g4 14.♗b4** 14.♖e1 ♗e2 15.♖e2 ♕d4 −+. **14...♖e2 15.♕e2 ♗e2 16.♔e2 ♕g4!** and the attack soon retrieves the lost material with interest.

The game Dmitrov–Spraggett continued (instead of 9...♗b4!) with 9...b5!? 10.cb5 ♗b4 11.♔f2 ♕b5 12.♘e2 0-0 13.♘a3 ♕b7 14.♘c2 c5 (Donaldson prefers 14...♗d6 15.♗f4 ♖ad8) 15.♘b4 ♕b4 16.♕d2 ♕b6 17.dc5 ♕c5 18.♘d4 ♖fd8 19.♖d1 ♕b6 20.♔g1?? (20.♗b2 ≅) 20...♖d4!, 0-1 (21.♕d4 ♖d8 −+).

B221) 8.d5 White usually postpones this advance until after 8.♘c3, but the added options for developing the Black King's Bishop are not especially better than the transpositional ...♗b4. **8...♗f5 9.♘c3** and now:

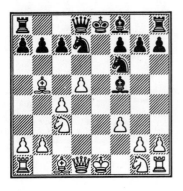

B2211) 9...♗e7 10.g4 ♗g6 11.f4! ♘e4 Instead 11...h6? 12.f5 ♗h7 13.h3 0-0 14.♗f4 +− was Polgar,J–Damaso, Oviedo rapid 1992. **12.f5 ♗h4 13.♔f1 ♘f2 14.♕e1! ♔f8 15.♘f3 ♘h1 16.♕h4 ♕h4 17.♘h4 ♘e5 18.♔g2 a6 19.♗a4 ♘f2**

20.♔f2 ♘g4 21.♔g3 ♗h5 22.♗f4 +−.

B2212) 9...♗c5 10.♕e2 ♕e7 11.g4 ♗d3 12.♕e7 ♗e7 13.♗f4 0-0-0 14.0-0-0 ♗g6 15.♘h3 15.♗a4! ±. **15...♘b6 16.♘a4 ♘a8 17.♘c3 ♘b6 18.♘a4, 1/2-1/2!** was Renet–Galego, European Cup 1994.

B2213) 9...♗b4(!) 10.♕e2?! Better is 10.♘e2! – see the B2232) 9.d5 line. **10...♔f8 11.♗e3 ♘c5 12.0-0-0 ♕d6 13.g4 ♗g6 14.♘h3 a6 15.♘f4** If 15.♗f4!? ♕b6 16.♖he1 (△ 17.♕e7 and 18.♕e8), Black defends e7 with 16...♘b3! 17.ab3 ab5, and the threat of 18...♖a1 and 19...♕d4 forces mate. If 18.♗e3 ♕a5 19.♔d2, then 19...♕a2! is lights out. **15...♗c3 16.♘g6 hg6 17.♗c5 ♕c5 18.♗a4 b5 −+** Rohl–Vitor, Venezuela-Portugal match 1995

B222) 8.c5 White plays to shut out Black's dark-squared Bishop at the cost of a backward pawn. **8...c6 9.♗d3** The alternative 9.♗a4 tends to discourage the plan of ...b6, but Black can switch plans with 9...♘d5! 10.♘c3 ♕h4 11.g3 ♕h5 12.♘d5 ♗d5 13.♕e2 ♗e7 14.♔f2 ♘f8 15.♗b3 ♘e6 16.♗e3

♗f6 17.♖d1 0-0-0 ∓ Diaz–W.Sariego, Cuba 1995. **9...b6** Deserving tests is 9...♘d5!?, △ 10...♕h4, as in the example above. The Black King's Bishop can become active at f6 or even c5(!) as in the line 10.♘e2 ♕h4 11.g3 ♕h3 12.♔f2 ♘c5! 13.dc5 ♗c5 14.♔e1 ♕g2 15.♖f1 0-0-0 −+. A massive strike will soon be underway on the two open central files. **10.cb6 ♕b6 11.♘e2 c5** 11...♗b4 12.♘bc3 c5 13.a3! ±. This can also occur by transposition in the line 8.♘c3 ♗b4 9.c5, etc.

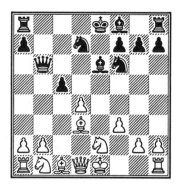

Two paths from the diagram:

1) **12.d5 ♘d5 13.♘a3 ♕b4 14.♗d2 ♕b2** 14...♕h4 15.g3 ♕h3 16.♕c2. **15.♘c4 ♕f6 16.0-0 ♗e7 17.f4** (Vitor–Santos, Portugal Ch. 1994) **17...♗f5! 18.♕c2 ♗d3 19.♕d3 ♘7b6 20.♘b6 ab6! 21.♕b5!** 21.♕d5 ♖d8 ∓. **21...♔f8** ∓.

2) **12.0-0 cd4 13.♘f4 ♗d6 14.♘e6 fe6 15.♕b3** (Shaked–Cukier, World Junior Ch. 1993) **15...♕b3 16.ab3 ♔e7 17.♗c4 ♖hc8 18.♖d1 e5 19.♗g5 h6 20.♗h4 g5 21.♗g3 ♘c5** =.

B223) 8.♘c3 ♗b4 If instead 8...♕e7!? 9.♘ge2 0-0-0 10.0-0 c6 11.♗f4 g5 12.♗g3 ♘h5 13.♗c6 bc6 14.♕a4 ♘b8 (14...♔b7 15.d5! cd5 16.♘b5 a6 17.♘d6 ♔a7 18.♘b5 =) 15.♗b8 ♔b8 16.♕c6 ♕b7 with an unclear ending which Black won in Vitor–Santos, Portugal Ch. 1992. After the text:

White can reply with either:

→ **B2231) 9.c5**
→ **B2232) 9.d5**

B2231) 9.c5 This seems less logical now that Black's Kingside Bishop is developed to b4. **9...c6 10.♗d3 ♘d5!** 10...♕e7?! 11.♘e2 0-0-0 12.♕c2! ♗c5 13.dc5 ♘e5 14.♗f5

♕c5 15.b4 ♕b6 16.♘f4 ♘c4 17.♗e6 fe6 18.♕b3 e5 19.♕c4 ef4 20.♕c5, 1-0 was Sax–Damaso, Benasque 1993. Spraggett recommends 10...b6!? 11.cb6 ♕b6 △ ...c5, as in the 8.c5 line. However, after 12.♘ge2 c5 13.a3 Black must part with his b4 Bishop (13...♗a5 14.dc5). **11.♘ge2 ♕h4 12.g3 ♕h3 13.♔f2 ♘c5! 14.♘d5 =** After the alternative, 14.dc5 ♗c5 15.♔e1 ♕g2 16.♖f1 0-0-0 ∞, Black's long-term attacking chances are quite good. The text led to a short draw in Ribeiro–Damaso, Portugal Ch. 1995: **14...♘d3 15.♕d3 ♗d5 16.♘f4 ♕d7 17.♘d5 ♕d5 18.♕e4, 1/2-1/2.**

B2232) 9.d5 ♗f5 10.♘ge2 0-0 Black's inferior Queenside position prohibits castling that way: 10...♕e7?! 11.0-0 0-0-0 12.♘d4 ♗g6 13.h4 ♗h5 14.♖e1 ♕f8 15.♘f5 ♗c3 16.bc3 ♔b8 17.♕b3 ♔a8 18.♗a3 ♘c5 19.♔h1 h6 (Yasseen–Ribeiro, Yerevan Olympiad 1996), and now simplest is 20.♕b4! ♘d3 21.♕f8 ♖hf8 22.♖e3 winning the Exchange; or 20...b6 21.♕c5! with a mating attack after 21...bc5 22.♗c6 ♔b8 23.♖ab1 ♔c8 24.♖b7! ♘d7 25.♘e7 ♕e7 26.♖e7 +- (△ ♗c5-a7, ♖b8#). **11.♗d7** Otherwise the d7 Knight will wander off and leave the b5 Bishop in an awkward spot. **11...♘d7 12.0-0 ♘e5**

No improvement is 12...♘c5 13.♘f4 ♖e8 14.♘ce2 ♕f6 15.♘g3 ♘d7 16.♔h1 ♗d6 17.♘gh5 ♕e5 18.g4 ♗g6 19.♘g3 ♘c5 20.♘g6 hg6 21.f4 ± Agnos–C.P.Santos (European Team Ch.), Pula 1997. **13.♔h1** Instead 13.b3? falls down a long, forcing variation: 13...♗c5 14.♔h1 ♘d3 15.♘g3 ♕f6! 16.♘f5 ♕c3 17.♗e3 ♗e3 18.♘e3 ♖ae8 19.♘c2 ♘b2 20.♕c1 ♖e2 21.♘a3 ♕f6 (△ 22...♕g6) 22.♖e1 ♖fe8 23.♖e2 ♖e2 24.♘b5 ♘d3 25.♕f1 ♕e5 26.♘c7 (26.♖b1 a6! 27.♘d4 ♖d2 -+) 26...♘e1! 27.f4 ♕e4 -+. So far we have followed Votava–F.Ribeiro, Yerevan Olympiad 1996, where Black could have equalized with **13...♘c4! 14.♕d4 ♗c3 15.bc3 b5 16.♘g3 ♗g6 17.f4 f6 =.**

Chapter Three
The Positional 4.♘f3

1.e4 d5 2.ed5 ♘f6 3.d4 ♗g4 4.♘f3

This is the classically correct move, neither weakening (4.f3) nor exchanging pieces (4.♗e2) when White enjoys a space advantage. Black's best chance is to challenge the center with a timely ...e5 once his Queenside development is completed.

Black's Portuguese response is **4...♕d5!** The move 4...♘d5 transposes to well known lines which Black was presumably trying to avoid by playing 3...♗g4. After 4...♘d5 White can obtain a slight pull with 5.♗e2 e6 6.♘e5, although he has sharper lines. After 4...♕d5 we consider the replies:

→ A) 5.♘c3
→ B) 5.♗e2

Instead, **5.♘db2** cedes too much central initiative to Black after **5...♘c6** Now 6.♗c4?! ♕h5 7.c3 0-0-0 8.b4 e5! 9.b5 ♘a5 10.♗e2 ed4 11.cd4 ♘d5 and Black stood much better in Ramik–Hausner, Czech Ch. 1994. Slightly better is **6.c4 ♕a5! 7.d5** Or 7.♗e2 ♗f3 8.♗f3 ♘d4 9.♗b7 ♖b8 10.♗f3 e5 11.0-0 ♗e7 ∓. **7...♘e5 8.♕b3** If 8.♗e2 ♗f3. **8...♘f3 9.gf3 ♗c8** ∓.

A) 5.♘c3 Usually this transposes to B) 5.♗e2; here we consider the lines with independent significance:

→ A1) 5...♕h5
→ A2) 5...♕f5(!)

Note that the reply 5...♕a5 at once transposes into the historic main line of the Center Counter (with 2...♕d5), when 6.h3 requires either 6...♗f3 giving White the Bishop pair, or 6...♗h5 yielding a big initiative after 7.g4 ♗g6 8.♘e5.

A1) 5...♕h5 We will examine two possibilities from the diagram shown on the next page:

White may consider:

→ **A11) 6.♗f4**
→ **A12) 6.♗b5!?**

Otherwise, **6.♗e3** is a placid continuation. After **6...♘c6 7.♗b5 e6 8.a3** a draw was agreed in Vorobiov–Ulko, Moscow 1996. For **6.♗e2**, see B2) 5...♘c6 below. There is no point in using a tempo with 6.h3 to force an exchange at f3, since Black will have to play it anyway. A game De Araujo–C.Santos, Argentina 1993 continued **6.h3 ♗f3 7.♕f3 ♕f3 8.gf3 e6 9.♖g1 a6 10.♗e3 ♘c6 11.0-0-0 0-0-0 =**.

A11) 6.♗f4 The purpose of this move is to make Black attend to his c7 pawn, so that he doesn't have time for the plan of ...♘c6 and ...0-0-0. **6...♗f3** Otherwise (say, on 6...c6) White will just play 7.♗e2, followed by 8.0-0 and h3 with advantage. Now, in return for

doubled pawns, White gets a space advantage and the Bishop pair. Based on the lackluster performance of Black's position, I must give the nod to A2) 5...♕f5 (preventing 6.♗f4!) for players who want to keep the draw in hand. After the text White can play:

A111) 7.gf3 c6 8.♖g1 g6 9.♕d2 ♕a5 10.♗c4 ♘bd7 11.♖g5 ♕b4 12.♗b3 ♗h6 13.♖g1 ♗f4 14.♕f4 0-0-0 15.0-0-0 e6 16.a3 ♕b6 17.♘e4 ♕c7 18.♕h4 h6 19.♖ge1 ♘h5 20.♕h3 ♘df6 = Lindberg–Olsson, Sweden 1996.

A112) 7.♕f3! ♕f3 8.gf3 c6 9.0-0-0 Or 9.♘e4 ♘bd7 10.0-0-0, transposing. **9...e6 10.♘e4 ♘bd7 11.c4 ♗e7** 11...0-0-0? 12.♘g5 ± Kobese–Fernandez, Moscow Olympiad 1994; 11...h6!?. **12.♖g1 0-0 13.♗d3 ♔h8 14.♖g2 ♖ad8 15.♔c2 ♘h5 16.♗e3** with a slight edge to White in Apicella–Ferreira, Asiago 1994.

A12) 6.♗b5!? An ingenious move to take away the option of ...♘c6. After **6...♘bd7 7.♗e2!** White regards the lost tempo as lost quality for Black's development. A similar interpolation is seen earlier in 4.♗b5 ♘bd7 5.♗e2, when Black's

Queen is blocked from recapturing the pawn at d5 (Chapter Four). **7...0-0-0** Less accurate is 7...e5 because of 8.♘b5!. **8.h3 e5!**

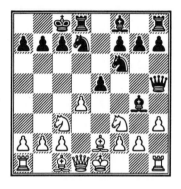

This thematic counterstrike loses force if deferred: 8...♘b6 9.0-0 ♗f3 10.♗f3 ♕h4 11.♗e3 e5 looks strong, but 12.♕c1! ♗d6 13.♘b5! (threatening 14.♗g5) forces 13...h6, when 14.♘a7 then wins a pawn. **9.0-0** Instead 9.♘g5?! loses momentum in an ineffective sortie against f7, which Black easily rebuffs: 9...♗e2 10.♕e2 ed4 11.♕h5 ♘h5 12.♘b5 ♖e8 13.♔d1 ♗c5 14.g4 h6! 15.♘f3 ♘hf6 16.♘bd4 ♖e4 17.c3 ♖d8 ∓ was Tan–A.Carvalho (Women's Olympiad), Manila 1992. **9...♗f3** The thematic sacrifice 9...♗d6!?? 10.hg4 ♘g4 fails because of 11.♘e4! f5 12.♘g3 +−. In positions where the White Queen's Knight is unavailable for Kingside defense, however, the same idea can be devastating. **10.♗f3 ♕f5 11.de5 ♕e5** Not

11...♘e5? 12.♗b7!. **12.♖e1 ♕a5** The position is approximately equal, with nothing for either player to get excited about.

A2) 5...♕f5 6.♗d3 This leads to equality at best. For 6.♗e2 see the B2) 5...♘c6 line. **6...♗f3** and now:

➛ **A21) 7.gf3**
➛ **A22) 7.♗f5**

A21) 7.gf3 ♕d7 8.♗e3 ♘c6 9.♗b5 e6 10.♕d3 a6 11.♗a4 ♗b4 12.0-0-0 ♗c3 13.♕c3 b5 14.♗b3 ♘e7 15.d5 ♘ed5 16.♗d5 ♘d5! 17.♕g7 0-0-0 18.♗d4 h5 19.♕g5 ♖dg8 20.♕d2 f6 ∓ and the Knight proved better than the Bishop in Prie–Galego, Linares (zt) 1995.

A22) 7.♗f5 ♗d1 8.♘d1 e6 9.♗d3 ♘bd7! This is Black's best try to squeeze winning chances from the position based on his more rapid development. He plans to castle long and play ...c5 with increased effect. Sterile equality results from 9...c5 10.dc5 (or 10.♗e3 ♘d5 =) 10...♗c5 11.♗e3 ♘bd7 (Ainn–Belanoff, IECC 1995) 12.♗c5 ♘c5 13.♗b5 =. On the other hand, 9...♘c6?! 10.♗b5 ♔d7 11.c3 a6 12.♗a4 ± lets White enjoy the benefits of his Bishop pair and little center (Borge–Tonning, Copenhagen 1996). After the text White has various ways to go wrong: 10.♗e3 0-0-0 11.c4 c5 12.♘c3? ♘b8! ∓, or 10.0-0 0-0-0 11.♗e3 c5 12.♘c3 cd4 13.♗d4 ♘c5! ∓. Perhaps best is **10.♗g5 0-0-0 11.♘e3 c5 12.dc5 ♘c5 13.♔e2**. At any rate, White is the one struggling to prove equality.

B) 5.♗e2

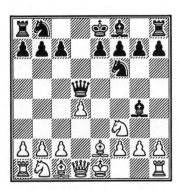

By far the most common continuation, leaving most options open. We examine:

→ **B1) 5...e6**
→ **B2) 5...♘c6**

Instead, **5...♘bd7?!** is too passive to put any heat on White's center, and unlike B1) 5...e6 it obstructs the Queen's retreat. A model game for White is Kranzl–Wandl, Vienna 1991: **6.0-0 0-0-0 7.h3 ♗h5**

8.c4 ♕a5 9.♘c3 c6 10.♗d2 ♕b6 11.♕a4 ♗f3 12.♗f3 e5 13.d5 cd5 13...♘c5 14.♕c2. **14.♘d5 ♘d5 15.♗d5 ♗c5 16.b4 ♗d4 17.♖ac1 ♘b8 18.c5 ♕c7 19.♕b3 ♖d7 20.b5 ♕d8 21.♗f7, 1-0**. Black's difficulty in finding a haven for his Queen bears a large part of the blame for this blowout.

B1) 5...e6 This quiet move fails to challenge White in the center. It usually leads to a Caro-Kann setup with ...c6 and (after a Queen retreat) ...♘bd7, often with Kingside castling. Black can also follow up with more aggressive ideas based on ...♘c6 and ...0-0-0, but if that is his intent I recommend B2) 5...♘c6 right away, so that he can play ...e7-e5 in one stroke. Without this central counter, White's superiority in that sector should allow him to turn aside any Kingside flank action. For his part, White should secure his space advantage by advancing c2-c4 before developing his Queen's Knight, so that Black cannot use d5 as a strong point. The possible drawback is that White's d4 pawn can be a long term weakness, so he is advised to overprotect it. After the text move, White can play as follows:

➔ **B11) 6.0-0**
➔ **B12) 6.h3**

Also possible is 6.c4!? ♗b4 7.♘c3
♗c3 8.bc3 ♛a5 9.♗d2 ♘bd7
10.0-0 0-0, 1/2-1/2 as in Lary–
Quaresma, Szeged 1994.

B11) 6.0-0 Moves such as 6.♘c3
and 6.♗e3 tend to transpose. After
White castles we consider:

➔ **B111) 6...♘c6**
➔ **B112) 6...♗e7**
➔ **B113) 6...c6**

B111) 6...♘c6 7.♗e3 0-0-0 8.c4

This position is often reached from
the move order with B2) 5...♘c6.
Here in lieu of ...e5 Black seeks
counterplay based on direct piece
pressure in the center, along with
the plan of ...h6, ...g5, ...♗f3 and
...g4. There is not much experience
with this treatment, but White

seems to come off better if he plays
accurately. Now we have two examples:

B1111) 8...♛d7 9.♘bd2 Vasic–
Djurkovic, Potoroz 1994, continued 9.♛b3 h6 10.♘c3 (10.♖d1!?)
10...♗f3 11.♗f3 ♘a5! (This only
works because Black's Queen is at
d7 instead of f5) 12.♛b5 ♛b5
13.cb5 ♘c4 14.b3 ♘a3 with better endgame prospects for Black.
9...h6 On 9...♗b4!? White plays
10.♘b3. **10.♘e5! ♗e2 11.♛e2
♛e8 12.♘df3 ♗e7** If 12...g5
13.♘c6 ♛c6 14.♘e5 ♛e8 15.f4!
±. **13.♘c6 ♛c6 14.♘e5 ♛e8
15.b4! ♗b4 16.♖ab1 ♗e7
17.♖b3** White has good attacking
prospects for this sacrificed pawn.

B1112) 8...♛f5 9.♘c3 On 9.♛a4
(A.Martinez–A.Carvalho, Women's
Olympiad 1996) Black has 9...♛a5!
stemming the attack. Otherwise if
9.♘bd2!? h6 ∞. **9...♗c5!?** A direct challenge which proved suc-
cessful in practice, but White can
improve. **10.♛b3**

(see next diagram)

In this complex position, White
maintains the better chances after
10...♗d4 Or 10...♘d4 11.♗d4
♖d4! (11...♗d4 12.♘d4 ♖d4

After 10.♕b3

13.♘b5! ±) 12.♘d4 ♗d4 13.h3!
♗e2 14.♘e2 ±. **11.♘d4** Better
than 11.♗d4?! ♖d4! 12.♘d4 ♘d4
13.♕d1 ♖d8 ⯈ in Rizouk–Rocha,
Algarve 1995. **11...♖d4** 11...♘d4
12.♗d4 ♖d4 13.♘b5! ±. **12.f3!
♗h5 13.♗d4 ♘d4 14.♕a3
♔b8 15.♖ad1 ±.**

B112) 6...♗e7 Black keeps the option to play ...c5. A game Schaefer–
Forchert in 1993 continued **7.c4
♕d8 8.b3 8.♗e3!?. 8...0-0 9.♗b2
c5 10.dc5 ♗c5 11.♘e5 ♕d1
12.♗d1 ♗f5 13.♗f3 ♗e4 =.**

B113) 6...c6 In the two examples I
have of this Caro-Kann treatment
White played 7.♘c3 here, but after
7...♕d8 achieved nothing with
8.♗f4 (Or 8.♖e1 ♘bd7 9.♘g5
♗f5 10.♗f4 ♗e7 11.♗c4 ♘d5 =
Korotkov–Ivashko, Moscow Ch.
1996) 8...♗e7 9.h3 ♗h5 10.♗g3

0-0 11.♖e1 ♘bd7 12.♘e5 ♗e2
13.♕e2 ♘b6 14.♖ad1 a5 15.♘e4
♘e4 16.♕e4 ♕d5 17.♕d5 cd5
and Black had better endgame
prospects in Villarreal–Soppe,
Buenos Aires 1995. Clearly, 7.♘c3
is not challenging enough. The
only way for White to seek an
advantage after 6...c6 is **7.c4!
♕d8 8.♘c3 ♘bd7**

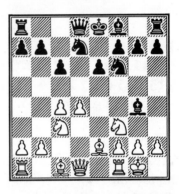

Curiously enough, we have transposed to a 3...♘d5 line which Capablanca briefly tried during the
first World War, before he took up
the Caro-Kann! A "normal" move
order would be 3...♘d5 4.♘f3 ♗g4
5.♗e2 e6 6.0-0 c6!? 7.c4 ♘f6
8.♘c3 ♘bd7. From the diagram
White has tried:

**B1131) 9.d5 ♗b4 10.dc6 bc6
11.♕a4 ♗c3 12.bc3 0-0!
13.♕c6 ♖c8 14.♕a6 ♘c5 ⯈**
Michelson–Capablanca, New York
1915.

B1132) 9.h3 ♗h5 branches further:

B11321) 10.♗f4 ♘b6 11.♕d3 ♗e7 12.♖ad1 0-0 13.♘e5 ♗e2 14.♕e2 ♘c8 15.♖d3 ⌂ 15.♖d2. **15...♕a5 16.a3 ♘d6 17.♗g5 ♖ad8 18.♖fd1 ♕a6 19.c5** Or 19.♖3d2 b5!. **19...♘f5** ⩱ Chajes–Capablanca, New York 1915.

B11322) 10.♗e3 ♗e7 If 10...♗d6 11.d5. **11.♘e5 ♗e2 12.♕e2 ♘e5 13.de5 ♘d7 14.f4** ± Vukovic–Popovic, Yugoslavia 1945.

B12) 6.h3 ♗h5 6...♗f3 7.♗f3 ♕a5 (Reyes–Chalker, Texas State Championship 1995) 8.♘d2 ±. **7.0-0 ♘c6** 7...c6 8.c4 ♕d8 transposes to the line considered above after 6.0-0 c6. **8.c4 ♕d7 9.♗e3 ♗e7** Probably better is 9...0-0-0, which is similar to line B111) 6...♘c6 above. Black may try to capitalize on the weakening effect of h2-h3, e.g. 9...0-0-0 10.♘bd2 h6 11.♘e5 ♗e2 12.♕e2 ♕e8 13.♘df3 g5 14.♘c6 ♕c6 15.♘e5 ♕e8 16.f4 ♘e4!, △ 17...♘g3. **10.♘c3 0-0 11.a3 ♖fe8 12.b4** ± White had a space advantage plus a solid position in Sepp–A.Martin, Orebro 1995.

B2) 5...♘c6!

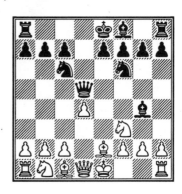

Both enterprising and correct. White has a variety of responses, which often intersect in a thicket of transpositions. White may consider a number of moves:

→ **B21) 6.0-0**
→ **B22) 6.♘c3**
→ **B23) 6.c4**
→ **B24) 6.h3**

B21) 6.0-0 0-0-0 7.c3 On 7.♘c3, best is 7...♕f5! 8.♗e3 e5 transposing to a good line for Black in B22) 6.♘c3, although the lines with ...♕h5 are not bad. On 7.c4, again I recommend 7...♕f5 – see the B23) 6.c4 line. The text is sturdy and unambitious. One thing to be said in its favor is that White recognizes the imminent danger to his center. We examine three choices for Black after 7.c3:

→ **B211) 7...♕h5!??**

→ **B212) 7...e6**

→ **B213) 7...e5**

B211) 7...♕h5!?? This led to a brilliant win in St.Amand–Vescovi, Bermuda Open 1997 after **8.♖e1?** e5 9.♗e3 ♗d6 10.h3 ♖he8 11.hg4 ♘g4 12.♕d2 e4 13.♗f4 ef3 14.gf3 ♘f2! 15.♗d6 ♖d6 16.♔f2 ♕h2 17.♔f1 ♖g6 18.♕g5, 0-1. However, the text move is based on an unsound sacrifice: **8.h3! e5!?** Otherwise, what's the point? **9.hg4 ♘g4 10.♗g5!** 10.♘bd2? f5! 11.de5 ♘ce5, △ 12...♖d2 -+. **10...♗e7** 10...♖d6 11.♘bd2. **11.♗e7 ♘e7 12.♘bd2 ♖d6 13.♘e4 ♖h6 14.♘g3 +−**.

B212) 7...e6 By exercising restraint in the center, Black hopes to initiate a Kingside pawn storm. The positional basis is that White's setup is geared toward a similar plan on the Queenside. **8.♗f4 h5**

4.♘f3

Also playable is 8...h6 9.♘e5 ♘e5 10.♗e5 ♗e2 11.♕e2 ♘d7 12.c4 ♕c6 13.♘c3 ♘e5 14.de5 ♗b4 =. The text is sharper, allowing fewer exchanges. Now against 9.h3, Black can ignore the "threat" and continue 9...♗d6! 10.c4 (10.♗d6 ♕d6 11.♘bd2 ♕f4) 10...♕f5 11.♗e3 ♘b4!? (11...♖h3 =) 12.♘c3 ♗f3 13.♗f3 g5 with good attacking prospects. **9.♘bd2 ♗e7 10.♕c2 ♖dg8 11.b4 g5!** Black has a good game. Kania–Gabrielsen, Copenhagen 1996 continued **12.♗c4 ♕d8 13.♗e5** 13.♗g5!? ♖g7 ⩲. **13...♗f5 14.♗d3 g4 15.♘e1 ♘e5 16.♗f5 ♘g6** 16...♘f3! 17.gf3 ef5 18.♕f5 ♔b8 19.♘g2 h4 ⩱. **17.♗g6 ♖g6 18.♘d3, 1/2-1/2.**

B213) 7...e5 A solid equalizer. If Black needs to win, however, he should take a chance on 7...e6 above. **8.c4!** Now Black's Queen is deprived of the desirable flight squares f5 and h5. **8...♕d7 9.d5 ♗f3 10.♗f3 ♘d4 11.♘c3 ♕f5**

(see next diagram)

The position is equal. We offer two illustrations from the next diagram:

After 11...♕f5

→ **B2131) 12.♗e3**
→ **B2132) 12.♗e2**

**B2131) 12.♗e3 ♘f3 13.♕f3
♕f3 14.gf3 ♘d7 15.♖fd1 g5
16.♖ab1 ♗b4 17.♘e2 f5
18.a3 ♗e7 19.b4 ♘b6 20.♗b6
ab6 21.♘g3 ♖hf8 22.♖d3
♖f7 23.♖e1 ♗d6 24.♖c1 h6
25.c5 bc5 26.bc5 e4 27.fe4
♗g3 28.hg3 fe4 29.♖d4 ♖f3
30.♖e4 ♖d5 31.c6, 1/2-1/2.**
Arencibia–Sariego, Matanzas
1995.

**B2132) 12.♗e2 ♗c5 13.♗e3
♔b8 14.♘b5 c6 15.♘d4 ed4
16.♗d4 ♗d4 17.♕d4 cd5
18.♗f3 g5 19.♖fd1 dc4
20.♕c4 g4 21.♗e2 ♘e4 22.f3
gf3 23.♗f3 ♘d2 24.♕c3 ♘f3
25.♕f3 ♕f3, 1/2-1/2.** Schild–
Liardet, Geneva Open 1995.

B22) 6.♘c3 A simple-looking
move, but in practice it is by no
means simple to deal with the pressure Black now generates on the
d-file. Black can answer with
either:

→ **B221) 6...♕f5**
→ **B222) 6...♕h5**

B221) 6...♕f5 If White cooper-
ates by castling Kingside, this gives
Black excellent counterplay with
...0-0-0 and ...e5. However, White
has a dangerous pawn sacrifice after
the immediate d-pawn push. In my
opinion this line is critical, with
Black struggling just to survive.

B2211) 7.♗e3 0-0-0 8.0-0 White's
play appears so classical and correct, with not a move wasted – how
can this be wrong? **8...e5!**

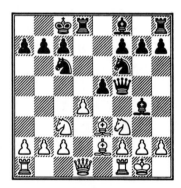

The problem is that White is ill-
prepared to deal with the challenge
to his center. **9.d5 ♘b4 10.h3**

1.e4 d5 2.ed5 ♘f6 3.d4 ♗g4

♗f3 11.♗f3 ♔b8! 12.g4?! Or 12.♖c1 c6 ∓. White is overextended. After the text, White quickly lost in Mortensen–Damaso (European Team Ch.), Debrecen 1992: **12...♕g6 13.♕e2 h5! 14.g5 ♘c2! 15.♘b5 ♘d4 16.♘d4 ed4 17.♗d4 ♕g5 18.♗g2 ♘d5 19.♕f3 c6 20.♖fe1 ♗d6 21.♖e4 ♗c7 22.b4 f5 23.♖e5 ♘f4!, 0-1**.

B2212) 7.d5! Now 7...♘b4 is our main line. Worth knowing are two lesser possibilities, which illustrate some interesting ideas:

1) 7...0-0-0? should have lost in Hjartarson–Galego, Oviedo (action tournament) 1992 by **8.♗d3 ♕h5 9.dc6 e5 10.♕e2** 10.♗f5! ♕f5 11.cb7 ♔b7 12.♕d8 ♗f3 13.gf3 ♕f3 14.♖f1 +−. **10...♗b4 11.♗e3?** 11.♗e4 +−. **11...e4 12.♗a6 ♕a5 13.♗b7 ♔b8 14.0-0 ef3** and Black went on to draw.

2) 7...♗f3 8.♗f3 ♘b4 Going for the c-pawn is risky because of the open c-file. After **9.0-0** we have **9...♘c2** 9...♕c2 10.♕d4 ♘a6 11.♗e2 ±; 9...0-0-0 10.♘b5! ♕c2 11.♕d4 ♕a4 12.♕c4 ♕a5 13.♗d2 e6 14.d6 c6 15.a4 +−. **10.g4! ♕g6 11.♖b1 0-0-0** 11...h5

12.♘b5. **12.♗f4 h5 13.♘b5 hg4 14.♗g2 a6 15.♘c7 ♕f5 16.♗g3 e5 17.♘a6 ♔d7 18.♖c1 ♖c8 19.♘b8 ±**.

Returning to 7...♘b4, White plays **8.♘d4!** Sterile is 8.♗b5 c6 9.dc6 bc6 10.♗a4 ♖d8 11.♕e2 ♗f3 12.♕f3 ♕f3 13.gf3 ♖d6 =. **8...♗e2 9.♕e2 ♕d7 10.0-0 ♘bd5 11.♘d5 ♘d5 12.♖d1**

White is richly compensated for the pawn, while Black has a long, arduous defense ahead. **12...e6** Better than 12...0-0-0 13.c4 ♘f6 (13...e5 14.♘b5! +−) 14.♗f4 ±. **13.c4 ♘b4 14.a3 ♘a6 15.b4 c5 16.♘f5 ♕c7 17.b5 ♘b8 18.♗b2 ♖g8 19.♗e5 ♕c8 ⊠**.

B222) 6...♕h5 Tried and true. This important stem position was reached as early as 1966! Black is ready to castle long, aiming as usual for the ...e5 strike.

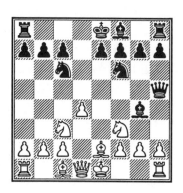

White may choose one of these:

→ **B2221) 7.♗e3**
→ **B2222) 7.♗f4**
→ **B2223) 7.0-0**

We may at once dismiss 7.♘b5? 0-0-0 8.c4 because of 8...a6 9.♘c3 ♘d4! 10.♘d4 ♗e2 11.♘ce2 e5, and Black stood better in Waters–Santos, Sas van Gent 1992.

B2221) 7.♗e3 0-0-0 8.h3 e5 9.♖g1?! This move looks, and is, artificial. **9...ed4!** An improvement over Cao–Damaso, Moscow Olympiad 1994, which continued 9...♘d4?! 10.♗d4 ♗f3 11.♗f3 ♕g5 12.♗b7 ♔b7 13.♕f3 c6 14.♗e3 ♕g6 15.♕e2 ♘d5 16.♘d5 ♖d5 17.♕c4 ♕d6 18.♔e2 ±. After the text move Black stands better: **10.hg4 ♕c5 11.♘d4 ♘d4 12.♗d3 ♕b6 ∓**; or **10.♘d4 ♗e2 11.♘ce2 ♗c5 12.c3 ♖he8 ∓**.

B2222) 7.♗f4 0-0-0 8.♕d2 e5!

This central counterstrike is a cornerstone of the Portuguese. Here it gains in psychological impact from the fact that White has not castled. The text is an improvement over 8...e6 9.h3 ♘e7 10.♗h2 ♗f3 11.♗f3 ♕a5 12.0-0 ± De Vreugt–D.Ribeiro, Baile Herculane 1994. **9.♗e5** The capture 9.♘e5 ♖d4! is too accommodating. **9...♗b4** Or 9...♗c5!? 10.♕f4!. **10.♗f6** Not 10.0-0-0? losing the Exchange by force: 10...♘e5 11.♘e5 ♗c3! 12.♗g4 ♘g4 (This is even stronger if White has castled Kingside!) 13.♕c3 (13.bc3 ♘e5) 13...♘f2 −+. **10...gf6 11.0-0** On 11.a3, Black plays 11...♗c5. **11...♖he8!** It is not easy to see how White will prevent a dangerous Exchange sacrifice at e2. Certainly 12.h3? ♗h3! 13.gh3?? ♕h3 −+ is not an option.

B2223) 7.0-0 0-0-0 8.h3

Now Black can safely equalize with 8...♘d4. If Black wants to play for a win, he can try the speculative **8...e5!?** when there may follow:

1) **9.hg4!? ♘g4 10.d5 ♘d4 11.♖e1 f5!** 11...♗c5 12.♘e4 ♖d5 13.♗c4! +-. **12.♗e3 ♘f3 13.♗f3 ♕h2 14.♔f1 ♘e3 15.♖e3 e4 16.♘e4 fe4 17.♗e4 ♗c5 18.♕g4 ♔b8 19.♖h3 ♕e5 20.c3 h5 21.♕e2 g5,** and in view of the volatile Kingside situation, Black has good compensation for his pawn.

2) **9.d5 ♗f3** 9...♗c5? 10.hg4 ♘g4 11.♘h4 ± G.Garcia–Damaso, Capablanca Memorial 1991. **10.♗f3 ♕g6 11.♖e1 ♗b4 12.♗d2 ♘d4 13.♖e5 ♘f3 14.♕f3 ♕c2 15.♕f4 ♗c3 16.♗c3 ♘d5 17.♕g4 ♔b8 18.♕g7 ♘c3 19.bc3 ♕g6 =** May–Dorner, 1966.

Returning to **8...♘d4** from the last diagram, White can play **9.♘d4** Not 9.hg4? ♘g4 10.♗f4 ♘f3 11.♗f3 ♖d1 12.♖ad1 e6 ∓. **9...♗e2 10.♘ce2** Speculative is 10.♕e2 ♖d4 11.♕h5 ♘h5 12.♘b5 ♖a4, while 11.♕e3 e5 12.♘b5 ♖d1! is good for Black: 13.g4? ♘g4! 14.hg4 ♕g4 15.♕g3 ♖f1 16.♔f1 ♕d1, 0-1 (17.♔g2 ♕d5) was Keitlinghaus–Zvara, Budejovice Open 1995; or 13.♘a7 ♔b8 14.♘b5 ♖f1 15.♔f1 ♗c5 16.♕d3 ♔c8 ∓. **10...e5 11.♗e3** Also 11.c3 ed4 12.cd4 ♗d6 13.♘c3, 1/2-1/2 was Bosch–Martinez, 1996. **11...♗c5 12.c3 ed4** Black could also temporize with 12...♖he8. **13.♘d4 ♕g6 =** Tinture–Brebion, correspondence 1992.

B23) 6.c4

A serious bid for a space advantage, which has the added benefit of letting White's Queen out of the box. However, if Black removes his

Queen from the d-file and follows with ...e5, his pieces can work around White's center very nicely and stir up trouble on the Kingside. Black can reply:

→ **B231) 6...♕d7?!**
→ **B232) 6...♕h5**
→ **B233) 6...♕f5!**

B231) 6...♕d7?! Compared to moving off the d-file, this retreat reduces the impact of having a Rook at d8 "smiling" at White's Queen (after ...0-0-0) – for instance, the d4 pawn may capture with impunity. Seeing that the central pressure is less, the result tends to be a cramped game for Black. **7.d5** More reserved is 7.♗e3 0-0-0 8.♘bd2 e6 9.0-0 ♗b4!? (9...♗e7 10.♘e5? ♗e2 11.♕e2 ♘d4 ∓ was Kassis–Vandevoort, Belfort 1989) 10.♘b3 ♖he8 11.a3 ♗d6 12.♘bd2 e5 13.d5 ♘d4 14.♗d4 ed4 15.♘d4 ♗e2 16.♘e2 ♕g4 17.♘g3 ♕f4 18.♕c2 ♖e2 19.♖ad1 ♘e4 20.♕e4 ♖e4 21.♘de4 ♗e5 22.b3 h5 23.♖fe1 f5? (23...h4 24.♘f1 g5 ∓) 24.♘c5 ♗d4 25.♘e6 ♕f2, 1/2-1/2 as in C.Burford–Chalker, Houston 1996. **7...♗f3 8.♗f3** It's worth digressing a bit to look at 8.gf3!? ♘e5 9.f4, seen in the next diagram:

9...♘g6 (Or 9...♘eg4 10.♘c3 g6 11.h3 ♘h6 12.♗e3 ♘f5 13.♕d2 ♗g7 14.0-0-0 0-0 with a solid but cramped position for Black) 10.♘c3 e6 11.de6 ♕e6 12.♗e3 (12.♕c2 0-0-0!, △ 13.f5 ♕c6) 12...♕f5 (12...♗d6? 13.c5!; 12...c6!? 13.♕c2 ♘h4) 13.♗f3 c6 14.♕d4 ♗b4 15.0-0-0 ♗c3 (15...0-0 16.♘e4 ±) 16.♕c3 0-0. The weakness of White's double f-pawns appears to balance the power of his Bishop pair, but I can't get too excited about Black's position. Continuing after the text move 8.♗f3, we have **8...♘e5 9.♗e2 e6 10.♕b3 ♗c5 11.♗e3 ♗e3 12.♕e3 ♘g6 13.♘c3 0-0 14.de6 ♕e6 15.♕e6 fe6 16.0-0-0 ±** seen in Okhotnik–Jadoul, Cappelle la Grande 1989.

B232) 6...♕h5 A tricky placement. Black obtains good play – unless White immediately pushes his d-pawn. We consider:

1.e4 d5 2.ed5 ♘f6 3.d4 ♗g4

→ **B2321) 7.♗e3**
→ **B2322) 7.0-0**
→ **B2323) 7.d5**

B2321) 7.♗e3 0-0-0 Now 8.♘c3 is the main continuation, considered below. For 8.0-0, see the B2223) 7.0-0 line. As before, the idea **8.h3 e5 9.♖g1?!** (Or 9.0-0 e4!) is artificial and not to be recommended. Two examples of this sideline:

1) **9...ed4** led to a draw in Manhardt–M.Cukier, World Junior 1996 although it required a little cooperation from White with **10.hg4 ♕a5 11.♗d2 ♗b4 12.♗d3 ♘g4 13.♔f1 ♕h5 14.♕c2 g6 15.♗b4?** White misses 15.a3! ♗d2 16.♘bd2 ±. **15...♘b4 16.♕b3 ♖he8!** **17.♘bd2** 17.♕b4?? ♘h2 18.♘h2 ♕d1 and mate next. **17...♕h4!** with perpetual check.

2) **9...♗f3!** Black need not sacrifice a piece to take advantage of White's awkward King placement. **10.♗f3 ♕g6! 11.d5** Instead 11.♗c6 bc6 has only a cosmetic effect after 12.d5 cd5 13.♕a4 d4 14.♕a6 ♔d7 15.♕b5 ♔e6 16.♗c1 ♗d6 ∓. **11...♘b4 12.♘a3 ♘d3 13.♔f1 ♘b2 14.♕b3 ♗a3 15.♕a3**, and Black can either steer for a better ending with 15...♕d3, or he can go whole hog with **15...♘c4! 16.♕a7 ♕d3 17.♗e2 ♘e3 18.fe3 ♕f5 19.♔e1 ♖d5!! 20.♕a8 ♔d7 21.♕h8 ♕g5! 22.♕f8 ♕e3** and White is lost, e.g. 23.♔f1 ♕f4 24.♗f3 ♘h5! 25.♕a3 e4 −+; or **23.♕f7 ♔c8 24.♔f1 ♕f4 25.♔e1 25.♗f3 ♕c4! −+. 25...♕d4 26.♕f8 ♖d8 27.♕d8 ♕d8 28.♖d1 ♕e7 −+.**

Returning to **8.♘c3**, Black continues **8...e5 9.d5 e4 10.♘d4 ♘e5 11.♕a4** Or 11.♗g4 ♘fg4 12.♕a4? ♘d3 13.♔d2 ♘b2 14.♕b5? ♘e5! −+ as in Grabbner–Forster, Liechtenstein 1997. **11...♗e2 12.♘de2 ♘d3 13.♔f1 a6 14.♕c2 ♘g4! 15.♘e4 ♘e3 16.fe3 ♕f5 17.♘f4 ♕e4 18.♕d3 ♖e8 19.♕e4 ♖e4**, and with 20...♗c5 or 20...♖c4 coming next, Black regained his pawn with a slight pull in Martinez–Gouret, Paris Ch. 1993.

B2322) 7.0-0 0-0-0 8.♗e3 Not 8.d5? ♘e5 9.♘bd2 e6 10.h3 ♗f3 11.♘f3 ed5 12.cd5 ♘d5 ∓ as in Horvath–Vandevoort, Arnheim 1987. **8...e5 9.h3 e4 10.hg4 ♘g4 11.♘bd2** Safer is 11.♘h4(!), when Black has just enough play to force a draw, e.g. 11...f5 12.♗g4 (12.g3 g5) 12...fg4 13.g3 g5 14.♘f5 ♘e5 15.♘d2 ♘f3 16.♘f3 ef3 17.♗c1 ♕h3 18.♘e3 ♖e8 19.♕c2 ♖e3 20.fe3 ♕g3 =. **11...ef3 12.♘f3 ♗c5 13.♗f4** Freeing the Knight to threaten 14.♘h2, so Black's reply is forced. **13...f5 14.d5**

14...♖he8! The idea is to follow up with 15...♖e4. An unnecessary pawn sac is the murky 14...g5!? 15.♘g5! (Preferable to 15.♗g5 ♘d4 16.♗f4 ♘e2 17.♕e2 ♖de8 18.♕d2 ♖e4 =) 15...♘d4 16.♗g4 fg4 17.♗e3 ♗d6 (17...♖d6? 18.♗d4 ♖h6 19.♘h3 ♗d4 20.♕d4 ♖g8 [Murgia–Gabetto, 1996] 21.♕a7 +−) 18.g3 ♘f5

19.♗d2 ♖de8 (19...♗c5 20.♔g2) 20.♔g2 ♕g6 21.♘e6 ♗e5 22.♗f4 ±. Returning to 14...♖he8! play may continue **15.a3** 15.b4 ♘b4 ∓; 15.♕c2 ♘b4 16.♕d2 ♖e4 17.a3 ♘c2! 18.♖ac1 ♘ce3!! −+. **15...♖e4 16.♕d2 ♘d4 17.♘d4 ♖d4 18.♕c1 ♖e8** ∓. White drops the c-pawn after 19.♗g4 ♕g4, and on 19.♗f3 g5 his dark-squared Bishop gets swamped – another reason for Black to hold on to his g-pawn four moves earlier!

B2323) 7.d5 This disrupts Black's normal plan of development, but with best play it should be no better than equal. **7...♘e5**

Premature is 7...0-0-0 8.♕a4 ♘e5 9.♘e5 ♗e2 10.♗f4 ♘g4 11.♘c6 bc6 12.♕a6 ♔b8 13.dc6 +−. **8.♘bd2** Objectively best seems to be 8.♘e5 ♕e5 9.♘c3 ♗e2 10.♕e2 ♕e2 11.♔e2 0-0-0 12.♗f4 a6 13.♖he1 (13.♖ad1 e6 14.de6 ♖e8) 13...e6 14.de6 fe6, and it will be hard for White to take advantage of the isolani at e6. **8...e6 9.♕a4 ♘ed7** The poor 9...♘fd7? leaves Black tied up after 10.h3 ♗f3 11.♘f3 ♘f3 12.♗f3 ♕e5 13.♗e3, when 13...♕b2 14.0-0 is clearly risky. Instead, the game Tumurhuyag–Hurelbaatar, Erdenet 1994 saw 13...b5!? 14.cb5 (14.♕b5!?) 14...♘b6 15.♕b3 ♘d5 16.♗d5 ed5 17.0-0-0 ♗d6 18.♕d5 ±. **10.de6 ♗e6 11.0-0** Or 11.♘d4 ♗g4 12.f3 ♗h3!, △ 13...♕h4. **11...♗d6 12.h3 0-0 13.♘d4 ♕g6 14.♘e6 fe6 15.b4** Black stands well after 15.♘f3 ♘c5. **15...a5! 16.ba5 ♕f5 =.**

B233) 6...♕f5! This has the advantage of supporting ...♘b4-c2 (or ...♘d3) in some variations. In addition, Black can exchange at f3 without loss of tempo. Now White gains nothing from 7.d5, e.g. 7...♗f3 8.♗f3 0-0-0 9.♕a4 ♘d4 10.♗d1 ♕e4 11.♗e3 ♕g2 12.♖f1 e5 13.♕a7 ♘d7 ∓. **7.♗e3** Or 7.0-0 0-0-0 8.♗e3 transposing, but not 8.d5?! e6 9.♗d3? ♗f3! 10.gf3 ♕h3 11.dc6 ♗d6 12.cb7 ♔b8, 0-1 (13.f4 ♘g4) as in Maric & Skripchenko–Hebden & Dunnington, France (exhibition) 1996. **7...0-0-0** We have reached the position shown next.

Two examples:

➔ **B2331) 8.♘bd2**
➔ **B2332) 8.0-0**

B2331) 8.♘bd2 e5 9.d5 ♘b4 10.0-0 ♘c2 11.♖c1 ♘e3 12.fe3 ♗c5 13.♖c3 (Poulton–Rewitz, Esjberg 1996) **13...h5 14.♕c1** If 14.♘b3 ♗b4 15.♖c1 ♕e4! and 16...♕e3. **14...e4 15.♘b3 ♗d6 16.♘fd4 ♕e5 17.g3 ♗h3** and 18...h4 with a strong attack.

B2332) 8.0-0 e5 For 8...e6 see B1) 5...e6. **9.d5 ♗f3 10.♗f3 e4 11.♗e2 ♘e5 12.♘d2** Or 12.♕d4 c5!. **12...♘eg4 13.♗d4 c5** Black has strong counterplay. Ellison–Conlon, Isle of Man 1995 continued **14.♗f6 ♘f6 15.♖e1 ♗d6 16.♘f1 h5! 17.♕c2 h4 18.h3 ♖de8 19.b4 ♕d7 20.♖ab1 ♖h6 21.♖b3 ♖g6 22.♔h1 ♖e5 23.♘d2, 1/2-1/2.** White was wise to make the offer, as after

23...♛f5! his defense is overwhelmed by 24.♚g1 ♛f4! 25.♘f1 ♜eg5 with a mating attack; or by **24.♖f1 ♛f4 25.g3 hg3 26.fg3 ♛h6 27.♚h2 e3! 28.♘f3 ♛h3!! 29.♚h3 ♜h5** with a forced mate.

B24) 6.h3

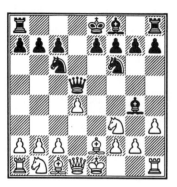

White pops the question to the Bishop at the most inopportune time for Black. If he retreats the Bishop, he deprives his Queen of the desirable h5 and f5 squares. We feel that Black's best choice is to cede the Bishop pair with 6...♝f3, and use the tempo saved to strike in the center with ...e5. Black can choose between:

➝ **B241) 6...♝f5**
➝ **B242) 6...♝h5**
➝ **B243) 6...♝f3**

B241) 6...♝f5 This move retains the Bishop pair, but does nothing to fight back in the center. Black tends to get a cramped game. **7.0-0** White should not block his c-pawn: 7.♘c3 ♛d7 8.0-0 (8.♝b5!?) 8...a6 9.♝e3 0-0-0 10.♝c4 g5 11.d5 ♝h3 12.gh3 ♛h3 13.♝e2 ♘g4 14.♝d4 ♜d6 ∓ was Agopov–Salmensuu, World Cadet Ch. 1996. **7...e6** Instead 7...0-0-0? commits Black to an untenable Queen placement at a5 after 8.c4 ♛a5 9.♘c3 e6 10.♝e3 ♛b4 11.♛c1 h6 12.a3 ♛b3 13.♜d1 ♝e7 14.♜d2 ♝g6 (Wolf–Virtual Chess [Harvard Cup], New York 1995 went 14...♘a5 15.♘e5 ♜hf8 16.d5 +−) 15.d5! ed5 16.cd5 ♘a5 (16...♘d5 17.♝d1 ♛c4 18.♘d5 +−) 17.♘d4 ♛b6 18.♘c6 +−. **8.c4 ♛d7 9.♘c3 0-0-0 10.♝e3** Compared to similar positions in B1) 5...e6, Black fares worse because he cannot threaten the center with ...♝f3. **10...h6 11.♛a4** White intends to follow up with 12.♜fd1 and 13.d5, and it appears that his attack will land the first blow.

B242) 6...♝h5 A difficult line for the defense, because White quickly gets a strong pawn wedge. Still, there is no clear refutation. **7.c4 ♛d6 8.d5 ♝f3** Or 8...♘e5 9.0-0 ♝f3, transposing. **9.♝f3 ♘e5 10.0-0 ♛d7** A finesse to gain a tempo, as White must defend his c-pawn. Black stands worse after 10...g6 11.♘c3 ♗g7 12.♖e1 0-0 13.♗f4 ♘f3 14.♕f3 ♕d7 15.♖ad1 ±, or perhaps ±. **11.♕e2** 11.♗e2!? e6 ∞; 11.b3 g6 =. **11...♘f3 12.♕f3 g6 13.♘c3 ♗g7 14.♖e1 0-0 15.♗g5 h6 16.♗h4 ♖fe8 17.♖ad1 a6 18.♗g3 ♕f5 19.♕f5 gf5 20.c5 c6 21.d6 ed6 22.cd6 ♖e6 23.♖e5, 1/2-1/2** was Mainka–Rogers, Prague 1992 (23...♖e5 24.♗e5 ♖d8 =).

B243) 6...♗f3 7.♗f3 ♕d7 8.c3 0-0-0!

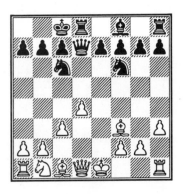

The most accurate move order. Black failed with 8...e5?! 9.d5! ♘e7 10.c4 ♘g6 11.♘c3 ♗c5 12.0-0 0-0 13.♗g5 ♕f5 14.♕d2 ♗d4 15.♖ac1 a6 16.♘e2 ♗b2 17.♖b1 e4 18.♘g3 ♗c3 19.♕c1 ♕e5 20.♗f6 gf6 21.♗e4 ± in de-Firmian–Vescovi, Bermuda Triangle 1996. **9.0-0 e5 10.♕b3** The main move, but White has also

tried 10.♗g5 with unimpressive results. After 10...ed4:

1) 11.♕a4? ♘e5 12.♕d7 ♖d7 13.♗d1 ♗c5 ∓ was seen in Fernandez–Vandevoort, Arnheim 1987.

2) 11.♖e1 ♕f5 12.♗f6 ♕f6 13.♗c6 ♕c6 14.cd4 ♗b4 15.♘c3 ♗c3 16.bc3 ♕c3 17.♕g4 ♔b8 ∓ was Leonardo–C.P. Santos, 1994.

3) 11.♗g4!? ♘g4 12.♗d8 ♘f2 13.♖f2 ♔d8 14.♕h5 f6 15.♘d2 ♘e5 16.♘e4 d3 =.

Returning to 10.♕b3, we have **10...ed4** Black gets overextended with 10...e4 11.♗e2 ♘d5 12.♘d2 ♕e6 (12...f5? 13.♘e4! ±) 13.♘c4 f5, when White can neutralize the pawn chain with 14.♘e3 ♘ce7 15.f3 ±. **11.cd4 ♘d5** Fedorowicz recommended 11...♕e6, although Black can hardly relish his endgame prospects after 12.♕e6 fe6 13.♗c6 bc6 14.♗e3 ♘d5 15.♘c3, e.g. 15...♘e3 16.fe3 c5 17.♘e2, or 15...c5 16.♘d5 ed5 17.♖fe1. **12.♘c3 ♘db4 13.♗c6** 13.♗e3!? ♘a5! (13...♘d4? 14.♗d4 ♕d4 15.♖ad1 ♕f6 16.♖d8 ♕d8 17.a3 ♘c6 18.♗c6 bc6 19.♕f7 ±) 14.♕a3 b6 15.♘e2! ♗e7 (15...♘c2 16.♕d3 ±) 16.♖ac1 ♖he8 ∞. **13...♘c6 14.d5 ♘d4!**

Fedorowicz–Galego (Marshall Chess Club), New York 1996 continued instead 14...♘e5 15.♕c2 ♘c4 16.♖d1 ♗e7 17.a4 ♘d6 18.♗e3 a6 19.b4 ♕f5 20.♕b3 ♘e4 21.♘e4 ♕e4 22.b5 with a strong attack on Black's King. **15.♕c4 ♘f5** One useful feature of this post is that it discourages White from playing ♗e3. **16.♗f4 ♗d6!?** This involves the promising offer of a pawn (16...♔b8 =). **17.♗d6 ♘d6 18.♕d4 ♔b8 19.♕g7 ♖dg8 20.♕h6 ♖g6 21.♕h5 ♖hg8 22.g3 f5 23.♘e2 ♖g5** Black has excellent compensation for the pawn, e.g. 24.♕h6 ♕b5, or 24.♕f3 h5 25.h4 ♖g4 26.♔h1 ♘c4.

Chapter Four
The Subtle 4.♗b5

1.e4 d5 2.ed5 ♘f6 3.d4 ♗g4
4.♗b5

This check usually transposes to the 4.f3 line in Chapter Two. Here we consider:

→ **A) 4...c6!?**
→ **B) 4...♘bd7**

A) 4...c6!? 5.dc6 ♕a5 6.♘c3 ♘c6 7.♕d3 For 7.f3 see Chapter Two, in the <u>B) 5.♗b5</u> line. There is only one game available with 7.♕d3, by no means a basis for definitive assessment. Gavrilov–Vlassov, Moscow 1996 continued **7...0-0-0 8.♗c6 bc6 9.♕c4 e5 10.f3 ♗e6 11.♕c6 ♔b8 12.de5 ♖c8 13.♕b5 ♕b5 14.♘b5 ♖c2 15.ef6 ♗b4 16.♔d1 ♖g2 17.♘c3 ♖d8 18.♔e1 ♗c4**

19.fg7 ♔b7 20.♗d2 f5 21.a3 ♗c5 22.b4 ♗b6 23.♘ge2 ♖g7 24.♗f4 ♖d3 25.♖d1 ♖f3 26.♖d2 ♖e7 27.♗d6 ♖e6 28.♔d1 ♗e3 29.♗c5 ♗d2 30.♔d2 f4 31.♖g1 ♖d3 32.♔c2 ♖f6 33.♘d4 f3 34.♘e4 f2 35.♖g7 ♔c8, 0-1. A truly insane game!

B) 4...♘bd7 Now White plays one of the following moves. Again, for 5.f3 see Chapter Two.

→ **B1) 5.♕d3**
→ **B2) 5.♘f3**
→ **B3) 5.♗e2**

B1) 5.♕d3 This dodge was tried in Navara–Buckley, World Cadet Ch. 1996. Perhaps the idea is to answer **5...♘d5** with **6.♕e4!?**, but in fact **6...♗e6!** intending ...c6, ...g6 and ...♗g7 is quite comfortable for Black (7.c4 c6! ∓).

B2) 5.♘f3 ♘d5 6.h3 ♗h5 7.♗e2 White has transposed to the classical 1.e4 d5 2.ed5 ♘f6 3.d4 ♘d5 line at the cost of a tempo (Ahn–Santos, European Junior Championship 1992). Black has equal play, being a move ahead in standard "book" lines.

B3) 5.♗e2! Paradoxically, this move shows some promise. White again steers for a ...♘d5 line at the cost of a tempo. The psychological value is that the Black Queen's Knight has been hoodwinked into going to d7, and the sharp character of lines with ...♛d5 is avoided. **5...♗e2 6.♛e2 ♘d5** Die-hard gambiteers may here explore 6...♘b6 7.c4 e6, which has a passing resemblance to other known ideas, but I cannot recommend it. White is consolidating easily after 8.♘f3 ♗b4 9.♗d2 ♛e7 10.de6 0-0-0 11.0-0 ♖he8 12.a3 ±. **7.c4**

Black can try one of these:

→ **B31)** 7...♘5f6

→ **B32)** 7...♘5b6

B31) 7...♘5f6 8.d5 This move prevents the development with ...e6, but Black gets a good game with the Kingside fianchetto. **8...g6 9.♘f3 ♗g7 10.♘c3 0-0**

11.0-0 ♖e8 12.♖d1 If 12.♗g5 e6 13.♛d3. **12...e5 13.de6 ♖e6 14.♛c2 c6 15.♗f4 ♛a5** Black had equality in Rocha–Santos (this and the next game reference were cited by GM Spraggett without date or place, and may have been training games).

B32) 7...♘5b6 8.♘f3 g6 Playable is 8...e6, since 9.d5 is parried handily with 9...♗b4 10.♗d2 (10.♘c3 ♘c5) 10...♗d2 11.♘bd2 0-0 12.de6 ♖e8. The text transposes to Pareira–C.P. Santos (the actual move order was 7.♘f3 g6 8.c4 ♘5b6). Play continued **9.♘c3 ♗g7 10.c5 ♘c8 11.♗f4 0-0 12.♖d1 c6 13.0-0 ♘f6 14.♗e5 e6 15.♘g5 ♘e7 16.♘ce4 ♘e4 17.♘e4** and White was better, although in pressing his advantage he lost through a faulty combination.

In summary, the unusual "tempo gambit" with 4.♗b5 and 5.♗e2! shows promise, and deserves more tests.

Chapter Five
White's Third Move

1.e4 d5 2.ed5 ♞f6

Most of White's alternatives are treated in the major works on the Center Counter. It is not my intent to duplicate or re-invent other sources, but to steer the reader to a line in which I have confidence. We will examine:

→ **A) 3.♞f3**
→ **B) 3.♝b5**
→ **C) 3.♞c3**
→ **D) 3.c4**

Of these, the most important is D) 3.c4, where we examine the Icelandic gambit.

A) 3.♞f3

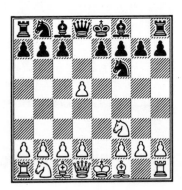

This subtle twist in move order might easily be dismissed as a trivial transposition to 3.d4 ♝g4 4.♞f3, but nothing could be further from the truth. Black's attempts to force a Portuguese-like position (when White doesn't cooperate) do not inspire confidence; I give them anyway for informative value.

For my money, I would fall back on transposing to one of the old main lines (i.e. 3...♛d5 or 3...♞d5). This volume is only intended as a supplement, so don't sell your old Center Counter books! We consider the replies:

→ **A1) 3...♝g4**
→ **A2) 3...♛d5**

Lacking independent significance is 3...♞d5 4.d4, which is the main line of the Modern Center Counter.

A1) 3...♝g4 If now 4.♝e2 then 4...♛d5 5.♞c3 ♛a5! (Black should avoid 5...♛d7?! 6.♞e5!, and 5...♛f5?! 6.h3. Instead 5...♛h5 6.0-0 ♞c6 7.h3! is A2) 3...♛d5 below). With 5...♛a5 we transpose to a branch of the old main line that is quite comfortable for Black after 6.d4 ♞c6 7.♝e3 0-0-0 8.♞d2 ♝e2 9.♛e2 ♛f5 10.♞b3 (Duras–Spielmann,

Vienna 1907) 10...e5! 11.0-0-0 ed4 12.♘d4 ♘d4 13.♗d4 ♗c5 =. Unfortunately, White can throw a monkey wrench into these plans with **4.♗b5!**

Neither of Black's replies has proved sufficient:

→ **A11)** 4...♘bd7
→ **A12)** 4...c6

A11) 4...♘bd7 5.h3! ♗f5 6.c4 a6 7.♗a4 Or 7.♗d7 ♕d7 8.0-0 e6 9.♖e1 0-0-0 10.♘e5 ±. **7...b5 8.cb5 ♘d5 9.d4 ♘b4** 9...ab5 10.♗b5 ♘b4 11.♘e5!. **10.ba6 ♘d3 11.♔f1 ♘c1 12.♕c1 ♖a6 13.♘c3 c6 14.g3 e6 15.♔g2 ♗b4 16.♗c2 ±** was Day–Kedel, Toronto Open 1995.

A12) 4...c6 5.dc6 ♘c6 6.♘c3 e6 7.0-0 ♗d6 8.♗c6 bc6 9.d3 ♖b8 10.♖b1 ♕a5 11.♘e4 ♗e7 12.♗f4 ♖d8 13.♕e2 ± was Grigg–B.Smith, England 1991.

A2) 3...♕d5 4.♘c3 ♕h5!? This is another attempt by Black to steer the game into Portuguese waters, but here again White has a nasty surprise. Of course, 4...♕a5 transposes into the so-called Venerable Variation with 1.e4 d5 2.ed5 ♕d5. **5.♗e2 ♗g4 6.0-0 ♘c6 7.h3!**

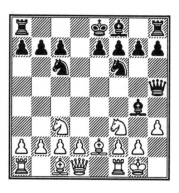

Now Black must either cede the Bishop pair along with any hope of initiative, or he must try an unsound piece sacrifice.

A21) 7...♗f3 8.♗f3 ♕f5 8...♕c5 9.♘e4! ♘e4 10.♗e4, △ 10...0-0-0 11.♕f3 ±. **9.d4!?** 9.♗c6 ±. **9...g5 10.♖e1 ♖d8 11.d5 ♘e5 12.♗e4 ♘e4 13.♘e4 ♗g7 14.c4 0-0 15.♕b3 h6 16.♗d2 b5 17.cb5 ♖d5?** 17...♘g6 ±. **18.♘f6 +−** from Nijboer–Vandvoort, Brussels (zt) 1993.

A22) 7...0-0-0!?? 8.hg4 ♘g4 divides further:

→ **A221) 9.d3**

→ **A222) 9.♘e4**

A221) 9.d3 e5 10.♘e4 ♘d4 11.♖e1 f5 12.♘g3 ♘f3 13.♗f3 ♛h2 14.♔f1 ♘f2 15.♛e2? 15.♔f2 ♗c5 ±; 15.♗b7! ♔b7 16.♛f3 e4 17.♛f2 +–. **15...♗c5 16.♛e5 ♘d3 17.♛f5 ♔b8 18.cd3 ♛g1 19.♔e2 ♖he8 20.♗e4 ♛g2 21.♔d1 ♛g3 22.♗f4 ♖d3 23.♔c2 ♛f2 24.♔d3 ♖d8 25.♗d5 ♛g2 26.♖e8! ♛f3 27.♔c4 b5 28.♔b5, 1-0.** Godena–Damaso, Lisbon (zt) 1993.

A222) 9.♘e4 ♘d4 10.♘eg5 ♘f3 11.♘f3 f5 12.g3 ♛h3 13.♖e1 e5 14.♗f1 ♛h5 15.♗g2 ♗c5 16.d4 ♖d4 17.♘d4 ♗d4 18.♗e3 ♗e3 19.♖e3 ♛h2 20.♔f1 ♘e3 21.fe3 ♛g3 22.♛d5 c6 23.♛e6 ♔b8 24.♛d6 ♔c8 25.♛e6 ♔b8 26.♛f5 ♛e3 27.♖e1 ♛f4 28.♛f4 ef4 29.♖e7 g5 30.♗e4 h6 31.b4 a6 32.a4 ♖d8 33.b5 ab5 34.ab5 cb5 35.♖b7 ♔c8 36.♖b5 ♖d4 37.♖c5 ♔d7 38.♗f3 ♖d2 39.♗e2 ♔d6 40.♖c8 ♔e5 41.♖e8 ♔f5 42.c4 ♖d7 43.♔f2 ♖c7 44.♗d3 ♔f6 45.♔f3 ♖e7 46.♖e7 ♔e7 47.♔e4 h5 48.♗e2 h4 49.♗g4, 1-0. Rowson–Vitor (World Junior Ch.), Halle 1995.

White may have found an ideal dodge to the Portuguese in 3.♘f3. At present it appears that Black has nothing better than to transpose to well known Center Counter lines with 3...♘d5 or 3...♛d5 4.♘c3 ♛a5.

B) 3.♗b5

An old "long line" with many labyrinthine straits. **3...♗d7** Old reliable. The trendy 3...♘bd7 has not convinced me of Black's compensation after 4.c4 a6 5.♗a4 b5 6.cb5 ♗b7 (Or 6...♘d5 7.♘c3 ♗b7 8.♘f3, transposing) 7.♘c3 ♘d5 8.♘f3 e6 9.ba6 ♖a6 10.0-0 ♗e7 11.♘e5 ♘5f6 12.d4 and White stands better (Finkel). After the text White has two good replies:

→ **B1) 4.♗e2**
→ **B2) 4.♗c4**

White gains nothing from **4.♗d7
♕d7 5.c4?!** 5.♘f3 =. **5...c6!
6.dc6 ♘c6 7.♘f3 e5 8.0-0
e4!** 8...♗c5 9.d3 0-0-0 ∓. **9.♖e1
0-0-0 10.♘g5 ♕f5! 11.♘f7
♗c5 12.♖f1 ♘g4 13.♘h8 ♘f2
14.♕e1 ♖f8 15.d4 ed3!**
15...♗d4? (De Riviere–Dubois,
Paris 1858) 16.♗e3!, △ 16...♗e3?
17.♕e3 ♘h3 18.♕h3 +–. **16.♘f7**
16.g3 ♕f3! –+. **16...♕f7 17.♗e3
♘h3 18.gh3 ♗e3 19.♔g2 ♕g6
20.♕g3 ♕e4 21.♖f3 ♘e5** –+.

B1) 4.♗e2 A positional treatment
that has never gone out of style.
**4...♘d5 5.d4 ♗f5 6.♘f3 e6
7.0-0 ♗e7**

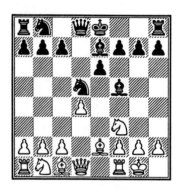

8.a3 On 8.c4 ♘b4 9.♘a3 0-0
10.♗e3, Black has several good
moves such as 10...♘d7, 10...c6,
10...a5 and 10...♘8c6 – all more or
less equal. For example, 10...♘d7
11.♕b3 a5 12.♖fd1 c6 13.♘e5?!
(13.♗f4 =) 13...♘e5 14.de5 ♕c7
15.f4 ♖fd8 ∓ was Tiefenbascher–

Wildner, Austria 1994. **8...0-0
9.c4 ♘b6** Black applies direct
piece pressure to the center, much
as in Alekine's Defense. The sim-
plifying plan with ...♘f6-e4 has not
put much of a dent in White's space
advantage. **10.♘c3 ♗f6 11.♗e3
♘c6 12.b3** Instead 12.b4 ♕d7
13.h3 ♖fd8 14.♖a2 ♘d4 15.♘d4
♗d4 16.♖d2 e5 17.♘b5 ♗e6
18.♘d4 ed4 19.♖d4 ♕e8 20.♕c2
♖d4 21.♗d4 f6 = was Lutikov–
Gipslis, Dubna 1976. **12...♕e7!
13.♕c1!?** On 13.c5 Black has
13...♘d5 14.♘d5 ed5 15.b4 a6
16.♖e1 ♖fe8 17.♕d2 ♗e4 = as in
Svidler–Tereshkin, St. Petersburg
open 1994. **13...e5!** It is best to
strike while White still has a Rook
at a1. If both sides double Rooks
(e.g. 13...♖fd8), then after 14.♖d1
♖d7 (14...♗g4 15.♘e4) 15.♖a2
♖ad8 16.♖ad2 White has a persistent pull. **14.de5** 14.d5 ♘d4.
**14...♘e5 15.♘d4 ♗g6 16.f4
♘d3 17.♗d3 ♗d3 18.♖d1
♗g6 19.♖e1 ♕d7.** Black has full
equality.

B2) 4.♗c4 ♗g4 5.f3 ♗f5

(see next diagram)

The retrograde 5...♗c8!? has come
and gone in popularity, but I prefer
to encourage White's weakening

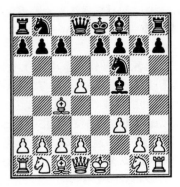

After 5...♗f5

push g2-g4. From the diagram we consider three moves:

→ **B21) 6.g4!?**
→ **B22) 6.♘c3**
→ **B23) 6.♘e2**

B21) 6.g4!? ♗g6! Most sources consider this to be an error. Obviously the move is more desirable than 6...♗c8 – if Black can only justify it! **7.♘c3 c6! 8.f4** White played 8.dc6 ♘c6 9.♘ge2 ♕b6 10.g5 ♘e5! 11.♗b5 ♘fd7 12.♘f4 0-0-0 ⩱ in Suetin–Korchnoi(!), USSR 1960. After the text, Black went astray in Shagalovich–Veresov, USSR 1961 with 8...h5? 9.f5 ♗h7 10.g5 ♘d5 11.♕h5 ♕d7 12.g6 fg6 13.fg6 ♕e6 14.♘ge2 ♕g6 15.♕g6 ♗g6 16.♘d5 cd5 17.♗d5 +–. The books have considered this to be case closed until now. Following 8.f4 we have:

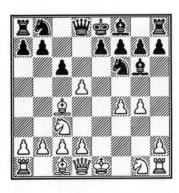

8...b5! 9.♗b3 b4 Black has good play, as the following examples show.

B211) 10.♘a4 ♗e4 11.♘f3 ♘g4 ∓.

B212) 10.f5 bc3 11.dc3 ♘d5 12.fg6 hg6 13.c4 ♘f6 14.♕d8 ♔d8 15.g5 ♘fd7! 16.♗e3 a5 17.a4 e5 18.0-0-0 f5! and Black's excellent pawns more than compensate for White's Bishop pair.

B213) 10.g5 ♘d5!? 10...bc3 11.gf6 cd2 12.♗d2 ♗e4 13.♘f3 ♗d5 14.♖g1 gf6 ∓. **11.♘d5 cd5 12.♗a4 ♘d7 13.♘f3 ♗h5 14.f5!?** 14.♗c6? ♖c8 15.♗d5 ♘e5!. **14...h6! 15.d4 hg5 16.♕d3 ♗f3 17.♕f3 ♕a5! 18.♗d7 ♔d7 19.♗g5 ♖c8 ∓.**

B22) 6.♘c3 ♘bd7 Reaching the position shown next.

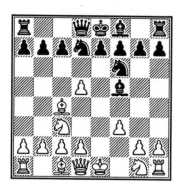

White may try one of these:

→ **B221) 7.g4!?**
→ **B222) 7.♘ge2**
→ **B223) 7.♕e2**

B221) 7.g4 ♘b6 8.♕e2 ♗c8
8...♗c2?? 9.♗b5 and 10.d3 +−.
**9.♕d3 g6 10.b3 ♗g7 11.♗b2
0-0 12.0-0-0 a6 13.♘ge2 ♘c4
14.bc4 b5! 15.♘e4 bc4 16.♘f6
♗f6 17.♕c4 ♖b8 18.♗f6 ef6
19.♘c3 ♕d6 20.♖de1 ♗d7
21.h4 ♖b4** ⩲ was Aronin–
Shamkovich, USSR 1959.

B222) 7.♘ge2 This common-sense
move, returning the pawn for a
space advantage, is the one most
likely to be encountered. **7...♘b6**
This position offers equal chances,
as our four examples demonstrate.

B2221) 8.♘g3!? ♘c4 9.♘f5
Murrey–Goldenberg, French Ch.

1991. **9...♘d5 10.♕e2 ♘cb6
11.♘d5 ♕d5 12.♘e3 ♕d7** =.

**B2222) 8.♗b5!? ♗d7 9.♗d7
♕d7 10.d4 ♘bd5 11.♘d5
♘d5** Or 11...♕d5!?, △ 12...0-0-0
and ...e5. **12.0-0** 12.c4!. **12...e6
13.c4 ♘e7 14.♗e3 ♘f5 15.♗f2
c6 16.♕c2 ♗e7 17.♖ad1 0-0**
= was Bouaziz–Larsen, Las Palmas
(zt) 1982.

**B2223) 8.♗b3 ♘bd5 9.♘d5
♘d5 10.d4 e6 11.0-0 ♘f6
12.c4 c6 13.♗e3 ♗e7 14.♘c3
0-0 15.♕e2 ♕a5 16.♗f2
♖fe8 17.♘e4 ♖ad8 18.♖ad1
♗g6 19.♔h1 a6 20.c5** So far
J.Gonzalez–S.Anderson, St. John
Open 1988. **20...e5** =.

**B2224) 8.d3 ♘bd5 9.♘d5 ♘d5
10.♘g3 g6!** 10...♗g6 11.f4 e6
12.0-0 (Spassky–Kudinov, USSR
1960) 12...♘e7! =; 10...♕d7
11.0-0 h5 12.d4 0-0-0 ∞.
Spassky–Banks, Canada 1971. The
text is Boleslavsky's idea. **11.f4
♕d6 12.♕f3 0-0-0 13.♘f5 gf5
14.♗d5? ♕d5 15.♕d5 ♖d5** ∓
was Fichtl–Karaklaid 1957.

B223) 7.♕e2 This has long been
considered Black's biggest hurdle
in the B) 3.♗b5 line. **7...♘b6
8.♗b3 ♕d7** Taking the d5 pawn

now would be premature, on account of 8...♘fd5 9.♘d5 ♘d5 10.♕b5. **9.d6!?** The stem game continued instead 9.d3 ♘bd5 = (Bogatyrchuk–Torre, Moscow 1925). That is probably White's safest route, given the analysis which follows. **9...♕d6 10.♘b5 ♕d7 11.♕e5 0-0-0 12.♘a7 ♔b8 13.♘b5 ♘fd5 14.a4 e6!?**

A suggestion by GM John Emms. Black seeks to make the best use of the exposed Queen position: before giving chase with ...f6 he waits for White to play ♘e2, taking away a good flight square from the Queen.

Earlier sources give 14...f6 15.♕e2 e5 (Not 15...♘f4? 16.♕f2 e5 17.♘e2 ♘e2 18.♕e2 ♗c5 19.d3 ♖he8 20.♘c3 ♗g6 21.♗e3 ♗d4 22.0-0 ± as in Royzhman–Shagalovich, Minsk 1961) 16.a5 ♘f4 (Better is 16...♘c8, Emms) 17.ab6 ♘e2, and it was long believed that

Black was winning, e.g. 18.bc7? ♕c7 19.♘c7 ♘d4 20.♘a8 ♗c2 21.♗c4 b5 22.♗e2 ♘b3, 0-1 as in Arning–Holtzhaeuer, corr. 1986. But Emms pointed out what would seem obvious, that after 18.♘c7! (△ 19.♖a8#) 18...♕c7 19.bc7 ♔c7 20.♘e2, Black can just resign, as he is down a piece and a pawn for nothing. An amazing case of mass hallucination.

After 14...e6!? in the previous diagram the position is relatively uncharted, but it looks very promising for Black: **15.♘e2 f6 16.♕g3 ♘b4 17.d3** Emms gives the accommodating 17.♘ed4 ♗c5 18.♘f5 ef5, when White's King is forced to live in the center. **17...♗c5 18.♘ec3 ♘6d5!** Creating a retreat for the Bishop. **19.♘e4** Or 19.d4 ♘c3 20.bc3 ♗c2! ∓. **19...♗b6 20.d4 e5!** White can now castle, but it will cost his material advantage: **21.0-0 ed4 22.a5!? ♕b5 23.ab6 ♕b6** ∓. The alternative, 21.de5 ♖he8! with an attack on the way, is even worse. Based on this analysis, the old long line with B223) 7.♕e2 has lost its poison.

B23) 6.♘e2

(see next diagram)

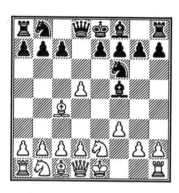

This position is not especially dangerous for Black if he is on guard against the plan of f4-f5. **6...♘d5 7.♘g3** Or 7.d4 e6 8.♘g3 ♗g6 9.0-0 ♘c6 10.c3 ♕d7 11.♘e4 0-0-0 = in Weglows–Witkowski, Poland 1975. **7...♗g6 8.0-0 e6 9.f4 ♘c6** Interesting is 9...♘e7!? 10.d4 h5! ∞ (Rabar), but considerably less so is 9...♘b6?! 10.♗b3 ♗c5 11.♔h1 0-0 12.♘c3 ♘c6 13.♘ce4 ± in Mieses–Marshall, Karlovy Vary 1907. **10.d4 ♘ce7!** Risky is 10...h5 11.c3 h4 12.f5!. **11.♗b3 h5 12.♕e2 h4 13.♘e4 ♗e4 14.♕e4 ♘f5 15.c3 ♗e7 16.♘d2 c5 17.♘f3 cd4 18.♗a4 ♔f8**, but Black had good play in Schmid–Bergrasser, corr. 1955.

C) 3.♘c3 ♘d5 4.♗c4 This is a quiet treatment that is usually classified under Alekhine's Defense, with the move order 1.e4 ♘f6 2.♘c3 d5 3.ed5 ♘d5 4.♗c4. **4...♘b6** Others include:

1) 4...e6 The previously solid reputation of this move has come under scrutiny from the surprising computer discovery that White wins a pawn by force with **5.♗d5 ed5 6.♕e2**, answering **6...♗e7** with **7.♕e5**, and 6...♗e6 with 7.♕b5. I have not been able to find any practice in this line, probably because it is non-intuitive rather than because of any intrinsic weakness. By contrast, normal development by White after 4...e6 poses no special problems, e.g. 5.♘f3 ♗e7 6.0-0 0-0 7.d4 b6 8.♘e4 ♗b7 9.♕e2 ♘d7 10.♖d1 c5 (Bisguier–Keres, Tallinn 1971) 11.dc5 ♘c5 = (ECO).

2) 4...♗e6 5.♕f3 c6 6.♘ge2 ♘c7 7.♗e6 ♘e6 8.d3 g6 9.h4 ±. Gundersson–Hlousek, Graz 1972.

3) 4...♘c3 5.♕f3 e6 6.♕c3 ♕g5 Or 6...♘c6 7.♘f3 ♕f6 8.♕f6 gf6 9.d4 ±. **7.♔f1 ♘c6 8.♘f3 ♕h5 9.d4 ♗d6 10.♗d2 ♗d7 11.♗e2** ±. Kholmov–Bohm, Moscow 1975.

Returning to 4...♘b6, White plays **5.♗b3 ♘c6 6.♘f3 ♗f5** Disregarding 6...♗g4? 7.♗f7 ♔f7 8.♘g5, Black's main alternative is 6...e5, which is both sharper and riskier because the White King's

Bishop remains with unimpeded activity. After 7.d3 ♗e7 White obtains an edge with 8.♘g5! (Instead of Grefe and Silman's 8.h3 0-0 =) 8...♗g5 9.♕h5 0-0 10.♗g5. One possibility then is 10...♕d4 11.0-0 ♕g4 12.♕g4 ♗g4 13.f4 with pressure against the f7 square. **7.d4**

Or 7.0-0 e6 8.d3 ♗e7 9.♖e1 0-0 10.♗f4 ♘a5 11.h3 ♘b3 = as in Estrin–Hazai, Agaard 1976. **7...e6 8.0-0** Also 8.♗e3 =, but not 8.♗f4?! ♗d6 9.♕d2 0-0 10.♗g3 ♗g4 11.0-0-0 ♘a5 12.♖de1 ♘b3 13.ab3 a5 with a strong attack in Lein–Alburt, New York 1980. **8...♗e7 9.♗f4 0-0** The sequence 9...♘a5!? 10.♕e2 ♘b3 11.ab3 0-0 12.♖fd1 c6 13.♘e4 ♘d5 14.♗e5 h6 = occurred in Mok Tze Meng–A.Wohl, Jakarta 1993. **10.d5** Rohler–Witke, Graz Open 1987 varied with 10.♖e1 ♘a5 11.♕e2 c6 12.♖ad1 ♘b3 13.ab3 ♘d5 14.♘d5 cd5 15.c4 ♗g4 16.h3

♗f3, 1/2-1/2. **10...ed5 11.♘d5 ♘d5 12.♕d5** Play is level, as two examples show:

C1) 12...♕c8 13.♘d4 ♘d4 14.♕d4 ♗f6 15.♗e5 c5 16.♕c3 ♗e5 17.♕e5 ♖e8 18.♕c3 ♕c6 = as in J.C. Diaz–Nogueiras, Havana 1992.

C2) 12...♕d5 13.♗d5 ♘b4 14.♗b7 ♖ab8 15.♘d4 ♖b7 16.♘f5 ♗f6 17.♖ab1 ♘a2 18.♘e3 ♗b2 19.♗c7 ♘c3 20.♗e5 ♘b1 21.♖b1 ♖fb8 22.♗b8 ♖b8 23.c3 a5 24.♘c4 a4 25.♔f1 g6 26.♘b2 a3 27.♖a1 ab2 28.♖b1, 1/2-1/2 was Masternak–Zolnierowicz, Wisla 1992.

D) 3.c4 This move is commonly played with the idea of returning the pawn: 3...c6 4.d4 cd5 is the Panov-Botvinnik variation of the Caro-Kann, and 3...e6 4.d4 ed5 is a form of the Exchange French which has gained in popularity in recent years. As these come under other openings than the Center Counter, we will consider only the lines where White accepts the gambit pawn:

→ **D1) 3...e6**
→ **D2) 3...c6**

3.♘f3; 3.♗b5; 3.♘c3; 3.c4

D1) 3...e6!? Black offers the Icelandic gambit. Now 4.de6 is the main line (see below), but we will pause to look at the relatively untested **4.♕a4** The game Navarro–C.P. Santos, Novi Sad (Olympiad) 1990 continued **4...♗d7 5.♕b3 ♘a6! 6.d4 ed5 7.♘f3 ♗b4 8.♘c3 0-0** 8...♕e7 9.♗e3 ♘g4 10.0-0-0 ♘e3 11.♖e1 ±. **9.cd5 ♖e8 10.♗e3 ♘g4 11.♗a6 ♘e3 12.fe3 ♖e3 13.♗e2 ♕e7 14.0-0** 14.♘e5 ♕h4 15.♔f1 ♖e8 16.♘f3 (16.♕b4 ♖8e5 −+) 16...♖f3! 17.♗f3 ♗b5 18.♘e2 ♕d4 19.♖d1 ♕f4 20.g3 ♗e2 21.♔g2 ♗d1 22.♖d1 ♕d6 ∓. **14...♗c3 15.bc3 ♖e2 16.♕b7 ♖e8 17.♕c7 ♖g2 18.♔h1 ♖e2 19.♕f4!** 19.♕a7 ♕d6 20.c4 (20.♕c5 ♕f4 −+) 20...♕g6 21.♖g1 ♗g4 22.♖af1 ♗f3 23.♖f3 ♕h5 −+. After 19.♕f4! best would have been 19...♗b5! 20.d6 ♕b7 21.♖ab1 ♕d5 =; instead the game ended abruptly with **19...♕e3?! 20.♘e5 ♕f4 21.♖f4 ♗h3 22.♘f7?? ♖e1, 0-1.** White would have stood better after the correct 22.♖g1 f6 23.♖f6 ♗g2 24.♖g2 ♖e1 25.♖g1 ♖g1 26.♔g1 gf6 27.♘c6 ±.

Returning to **4.de6**, Black answers **4...♗e6** reaching the position in the following diagram.

White has two responses:

→ **D11) 5.d4**
→ **D12) 5.♘f3!**

D11) 5.d4 In Grefe and Silman (1981) this was case closed: "... a disaster for Black." How things change! **5...♗b4** Now 6.♗d2 (analyzed below) is the only good move. For example, after **6.♘c3?! ♘e4**, White is in danger of being flattened by an overwhelming Black initiative: **7.♕d3** 7.a3 ♘c3 8.♕d3 ♕e7! 9.ab4 ♗c4 10.♕e3 ♗f1 11.♕e7 ♔e7 12.♔f1 ♘d5 ∓. **7...♗f5 8.♘ge2!?** Emms; 8.♕f3 ♕d4 9.♘ge2 ♕d7 10.a3 ♘c6 11.♗f4 ♘e5 12.♕e3 ♘d3 13.♔d1 ♗c5, 0-1 was Ruton–Hsu, Tunja 1989; 8.♕e3 0-0 9.♘ge2 ♖e8 10.♕f3 ♘c3 11.bc3 ♕d4! −+ 12.♗d2 ♕e5 13.♕e3 ♗c5 14.♕e5 ♖e5 15.♗f4 ♖e7 16.0-0-0 ♗a3 17.♔d2 ♘a6 18.♘d4 ♖d8 19.♖e1 ♖d4!, 0-1 was Thirion–Berend,

Eupen 1995. **8...♘c6!** 8...♘c3 =. **9.a3** 9.♕e3 0-0, △ 10...♖e8. **9...♗c3 10.bc3 ♘e5 11.♕d1 ♘g4! 12.♗e3 ♘e3 13.fe3 ♕h4 14.g3 ♕h6 15.♕c1 ♕c6! 16.♗g2 ♕c4** ∓. Black has excellent middlegame prospects based on his control of key light squares and White's backward pawn on the e-file. Returning to **6.♗d2** (after 5.d4 ♗b4), we consider:

➜ **D111) 6...♕e7**
➜ **D112) 6...♗d2!?**

D111) 6...♕e7 One of the old main lines of this gambit, which has been very good for Black in practice. We examine:

➜ **D1111) 7.♗b4**
➜ **D1112) 7.♕e2**
➜ **D1113) 7.♗e2**

D1111) 7.♗b4 ♕b4 Here we will focus on 8.♕d2, but worth considering is **8.♘d2 ♘c6!** and now:

1) **9.d5 0-0-0! 10.dc6** 10.de6 ♖he8 11.♗e2 ♖e6; If 10.♘gf3 see "2" below. **10...♖he8 11.♗e2 ♘e4 12.♘gf3 ♗c4** and White is bound to lose material.

2) **9.♘gf3 0-0-0 10.d5 ♗g4!?** Best is 10...♘d5! 11.cd5 ♗d5

12.♗e2 ♗f3 13.gf3 ♖he8 14.a3 ♕f4! and White has no good move against the coming 15...♘d4. The text is the historically important game A.Sokolov–Speelman, Madrid 1988. **11.♗e2** Missing 11.dc6! ♖fe8 (11...♘e4? 12.♕b3!) 12.♗e2 which leaves Black without a crisp continuation: 12...bc6 (or else 13.♕b3! is strong) 13.♕c2! ♖d7 (13...♘h5 14.h3!) 14.♔f1 ♖d2 15.♕d2 ♕d2 16.♘d2 ♗e2 17.♔g1 and Black has rather muddy compensation for the Exchange. **11...♗f3 12.♗f3 ♖he8 13.♔f1 ♘d4 14.♕c1 ♘f3 15.♘f3 ♖e4 16.b3 ♖de8 17.h3 ♘h5 18.g3 ♘g3! 19.fg3 ♖e3 20.♘g1 ♕d6 21.♖h2 ♖g3 22.♕b2 ♕g6 23.♔f2 ♖ee3 24.♘e2 ♖gf3 25.♔e1 ♕g1 26.♔d2 ♕h2 27.♖e1 ♕f2, 0-1**.

Returning to **8.♕d2**, Black continues **8...♘c6** with the following position:

Interesting is 8...♕e7!? 9.♕e3 (9.♕e2 ♕b4) 9...♘g4 10.♕a3 ♕f6 (10...♕h4 [Bednarski–Kolasinski, Poland 1994] 11.♕g3!?) 11.♘f3 ♘c6 12.d5 ♘d4 13.♕c3 ♘f3 14.gf3 ♘e5 15.♘d2 ♗f5 ∞ as in Doghri–Maljtin, Moscow 1991. **9.♘c3** Instead 9.♕b4 ♘b4 10.♘a3 0-0-0 11.d5 ♗f5 12.f3 ♖he8 13.♔f2 c6 14.g4 ♗g6 15.g5 ♘h5 16.♘h3 cd5 17.♗e2 ♗f5 18.♘g1 d4 19.♖e1 d3, 0-1 was Bauer–Klein, Germany 1994. Another game went 9.d5 0-0-0 10.♘a3 ♗f5 11.f3 ♖he8 12.♗e2 ♕c5 13.♔f1 ♘b4 14.g4 ♘fd5 15.cd5 ♘d5 16.♕c1 ♘e3 17.♗e1 ♗c2 18.♘c2 ♘c2 19.♔f1 ♖d5 20.♖b1 ♘e3, 1/2-1/2. Metz–Hauke, Germany 1989. **9...0-0-0** Perfectly good is 9...♗c4 10.♗c4 ♕c4 11.♕e3 ♔f8 12.0-0-0 ♘b4 13.♔b1 ♘fd5 14.♕d2 ♘c3 15.bc3 ♘d5 16.♔b2 ♖e8 17.♖e1 ♖e1 18.♕e1 h5 ∓ as in Doghri–Galego, Algarve 1995. **10.d5 ♗g4 11.f3 ♖he8 12.♗e2 ♗f5 13.0-0-0 ♘a5 14.g4 ♗g6 15.♘h3** Emms gives 15.b3 c6 as good for Black, and indeed it is: 16.♗d3 ♗d3 17.♕d3 b5! 18.cb5 ♘d5 19.♕f5 ♔b8 20.♘b1 ♖e1 (Black has a raging attack) 21.♕d3 ♕f4 22.♔b2 ♖d1 23.♕d1 ♕f6 24.♔c1 ♘b4 25.♕e2 ♘d3 –+. **15...♘d7!?** The plan of ...♘c5-b3 is highly annoy-

ing. Also strong is 15...♘c4(!) 16.♗c4 ♕c4, because White still has weak pawns: 17.♘f4 ♘d7 18.♘g6 (18.♖he1 ♘e5 ∓) 18...hg6 19.♖he1 ♖e1 20.♖e1 ♘b6 ∓. **16.♘e4** In Kujif–Hodgson, Wijk aan Zee 1989 White lost in short order with 16.♘b1? ♕b3!! 17.♗d3 ♕a2 18.♕b4 ♖e2! 19.♗e2 ♘b3 20.♕b3 ♕b3 21.♖d2 ♕e3!, 0-1. Emms suggests instead 16.♗d3, but 16...♗d3 17.♕d3 ♘c4 18.♕b1 ♖e3! gives Black an overpowering position. **16...♕a4 17.b3 ♕a3 18.♕b2 ♕b2 19.♔b2 ♗e4 20.fe4 ♖e4 21.♖he1 ♖de8 22.♘g1** White has held on by his fingernails, and he will soon play ♔c2-d2 relieving the pin on his Bishop. Since it will take a while for Black to bring his Knight at a5 into play, the prospects tend to level out.

In view of this line, the earlier alternative 15...♘c4! deserves consideration.

D1112) 7.♕e2!? This is a serious try, not to be dismissed lightly. **7...♘c6 8.♘f3 0-0-0!** An improvement on 8...♗d2 9.♘bd2 0-0-0 as in Vajda–Conlon, Bratislava 1993. Now instead of the meek 10.0-0-0? which returned the pawn for nothing, White comes out on top after 10.d5! ♘b4 11.♘b3 ♖he8 12.de6 ♕e6 13.♕e6 ♖e6 14.♗e2 ♘c2 15.♔f1 ♘a1 16.♘a1 ±. An over-the-board inspiration in one of my action games was 8...♗g4!? 9.♕e7 ♗e7, but Black's compensation after 10.♗e3 is unclear at best. **9.d5 ♖he8**

There is no practice in this position, but a few variations suggest that Black's offer of the piece is fully sound:

1) **10.dc6 ♕c5! 11.cb7 ♔b7 12.♘c3 ♗c4 13.♗e3 ♗e2 14.♗c5 ♗f1 15.♔f1 ♗c5 ∓**

2) **10.de6 ♕c5! 11.♘c3** Or 11.g3 g5! 12.♘c3 ♖e6 13.♗e3 ♕a5 14.♕c2 g4 15.♘d2 ♘d4 16.♕c1 ♕f5! 17.♔d1 ♖e3 18.fe3 ♘f3 −+. **11...♖d2! 12.♕d2** 12.♔d2 ♖e6 13.♕d1 ♘e4 ∓. **12...♖e6 13.♗e2 ♘e4 14.♕c2 ♕f2 15.♔d1 ♗c3 16.bc3 ♕e3** White is a Rook ahead, but he's in a heap of trouble, e.g. **17.♔e1 ♘c3 18.♔f1 ♘e4 19.♔e1 ♖d6 20.♖f1 ♘b4 −+.**

D1113) 7.♗e2 ♘c6 The sharpest, involving a piece sacrifice. Instead 7...♗c4?! only trades two minor pieces for a Rook, e.g. 8.♕a4 ♘c6 9.♗b4 ♕b4 10.♕b4 ♘b4 11.♗c4 ♘c2 12.♔d2 ♘a1 13.♘c3 0-0-0 14.♘f3 followed by 15.♖a1, and White stood clearly better in Belik–Weiland, Giessen Open 1991 and Gross–Weiland, Giessen Open 1995(!). On 7...0-0 best is 8.d5 ♗f5 9.♗b4 ♕b4 10.♕d2 ♕d2 11.♘d2 ♖e8 12.♔f1 ♘bd7 13.♘gf3 ♘c5 14.♘d4 ♗d3 15.h4 ♗e2 16.♘e2 ♘d3 17.♖h3 ±. Ortel–Dupsky, Zalakaros Open 1991. **8.d5 ♘d5 9.cd5 ♗d5 10.♔f1 0-0-0 11.♕e1 ♗d2 12.♘d2 ♔b8** Insufficient is 12...♗g2 13.♔g2 ♕g5 14.♔f1 ♕d2 15.♕d2 ♖d2 16.♖b1 ±. **13.♗f3** The exchange of Bishops eases White's development but leaves his light squares vulnerable. Nor is the alternative 13.♘c4!? free of problems: 13...♘d4 14.♘e3 ♗c6 15.♖d1 f5! 16.♕c3 ♘e2 17.♘e2 (17.♖d8 ♖d8 18.♘e2 ♕e4! ∓) 17...♖d1 18.♘d1 ♖d8 19.♕e1 ♕g5 20.f3 ♖d2 with excellent compensation for Black. **13...♕d6 14.♗d5 ♕d5 15.♘gf3 ♖he8 16.♕c1 ♕d3 17.♔g1 ♖e2**

18.♕c4!? Messy is 18.♘b3 ♖c2 19.♕f1 ♖b2 because White's a-pawn is going to fall next. The same goes for 18.♕c3 ♘e5! 19.♕d3 (19.♘e5?! ♕c3 20.bc3 ♖dd2 21.♘g4 f5) 19...♘d3 20.♖f1 ♘b2 ∞ (Gurieli). **18...♖d2 19.♘d2 ♕d2 20.♕c3** Thus far as in Ioselani–Gurieli, Tblisi 1987. Now Emms gives **20...♕c3 21.bc3 ♖d3 22.g3 ♖c3 23.♔g2 a5** with an equal ending.

D112) 6...♗d2!? 7.♕d2 ♕e7 8.♕e3 The clumsy 8.♕e2?!, blocking the Bishop's development, has led to predictable results after 8...♘c6 9.♘f3 0-0-0:

1) 10.d5? ♖he8! 11.♘c3 (11.♘bd2 ♕c5 12.0-0-0 ♗d5 ∓) 11...♗d5 12.cd5 ♕b4 –+.

2) 10.♘c3 ♘d4 11.♘d4 ♖d4 12.♕e3 ♕d7 13.♖d1? (13.♘e2 ♖c4 14.♕a7 ♖a4 ∓) 13...♖d1 14.♘d1 ♖e8 15.♕d2 ♗c4 and Black soon won a second pawn in Z. Polgar–D.Olafsson, Reykjavic 1988.

3) 10.♘bd2 ♘d4 11.♘d4 ♖d4 12.♖d1 ♖e8 13.g3 ♗g4! 14.f3 ♕b4 15.♕e8 ♘e8 16.fg4 ♘f6 17.♖g1 ♕e7 18.♗e2 ♘g4 19.♖c1

♕e3, 0-1. Prill–Gurieli, Baden-weiler Open 1990.

Back to 8.♕e3, there follows **8...♘c6 9.♘f3** Not 9.d5? ♘g4! 10.♕c3 ♗d5 11.♘e2 ♗e6 12.♕g7 0-0-0 –+ (Emms). **9...0-0-0 10.♗e2** Again, 10.d5? fails to 10...♖he8! 11.de6 ♘g4 12.♕e2 ♕b4 –+, or 11.dc6 ♘g4! 12.cb7 ♔b8 –+ (Emms). **10...♖he8 11.d5** Black's superior development was telling after 11.0-0?! ♗g4! 12.♘c3 ♗f3 13.♗f3 ♕b4 14.♕g5 ♘d4, with a strong initiative in Romily–And. Martin, Aberdeen 1991. After the text, Emms gives **11...♘b4!? 12.0-0!** 12.♘d4 c5! 13.dc6 ♖d4! –+. **12...♗d5!?** 12...♘c2 13.♕a7 ∞. **13.cd5 ♕e3 14.fe3 ♘c2 15.♘c3 ♘a1 16.♖a1 ♘d5 17.♘d5 ♖d5** with an equal ending.

D12) 5.♘f3!

The most solid continuation. Black may try one of the following:

➔ **D121) 5...♘c6**
➔ **D122) 5...♕e7**

D121) 5...♘c6 A natural move, leading to sharp play. Despite its early high-profile successes in the hands of GMs Speelman and Hodgson, I cannot recommend it unreservedly.

➔ **D1211) 6.d4!**
➔ **D1212) 6.♗e2**

A more restrained policy has tended to give Black good counterplay. An intriguingly unclear example from recent play is Onischuk–Thorhallsson, New York Open 1997: 6.d3 ♗c5 7.♗e3 ♗e3 8. fe3 ♘g4 9.♕e2 ♕f6 10.♘c3 ♕h6 11.♘d5 ♗d5 12.cd5 ♘b4 13.e4 0-0 14.♕d2 ♕b6 15.a3 ♘d5 16.ed5 ♖fe8 17.♗e2 ♕f2 18.♔d1 ♖e7 19.d4? (19.♗f1 ♖d8 20.h3 ±) 19...♖e2 20.♕e2 ♘e3 21.♔d2 ♘c4 22.♔d3 ♘b2 23.♔d2 ♘c4 24.♔d3 ♘b2 25.♔d2, 1/2-1/2.

D1211) 6.♗e2 Such staid development has tended to favor the second player. **6...♗c5 7.0-0 ♕d7** Now there may follow:

1) **8.a3 0-0-0 9.♘c3 ♖he8 10.b4 ♗d4 11.♗b2 ♗g4 12.♖b1 ♗f5 13.♖c1 ♘e4 14.b5 ♘e5 15.♘e5 ♖e5 16.d3 ♘f2! 17.♖f2 ♗f2 18.♔f2 ♕d4 19.♔f1 ♖e2! 20.♘e2 ♕b2 21.♖c3 ♗g4 22.♖c2 ♕a3 23.♖d2 ♕c5 24.h3 ♖d6 25.d4 ♖f6 26.♔g1 ♕e7 27.♕e1 ♕e3 28.♔h2 ♗h3!, 0-1.** Daniliuk–Ulko, Moscow Open 1995.

2) **8.♘c3 0-0-0 9.♘a4 ♗d4 10.d3 ♖he8 11.♗f4 ♗f5 12.♖e1 ♘g4 13.♗g3 ♘ge5 14.♘d4 ♘d4 15.♘c3 ♗d3** Brunner–Manor, Bern 1990. **16.♗e5 ♘e2 ∓.**

3) **8.b4!? ♗b4** Or 8...♗d4!?. **9.d4 ♗g4 10.d5** 10.♗b2 0-0-0 11.d5 ♘a5!, IM Andrew Martin. **10...♗f3 11.♗f3 ♘e5 12.♗b2 ♘f3 13.♕f3 0-0-0 14.♗f6** 14.♕b3!?. **14...gf6 15.♘c3 ♖hg8 16.♖ab1 ♗f8! 17.♘b5 ♗c5 18.♕b3 c6 19.♘c3 ♖g2 20.♔h1 ♖g6 ∓** was Weston–Bryson, Scottish Ch. 1994.

4) **8.d3 0-0-0 9.♘c3** 9.♗e3 ♕e7!. **9...♗f5 10.♕a4 ♗d3 11.♗d3 ♕d3 12.♗g5 ♘d4!?** 12...♕f5 ∓. **13.♘e5 ♕f5 14.♘f7 ♖df8 15.♖ae1 ♘d7 16.♘h8 ♕g5 17.♘e4 ♘f3! 18.♔h1**

♕h5 19.gf3 ♘e5! 20.♘c5 ♕f3, 1/2-1/2. Klinger–Einarsson, Dortmund 1987.

D1212) 6.d4! The insertion of 5.♘f3 ♘c6 before this thrust makes a big difference in White's favor. **6...♗b4 7.♘c3**

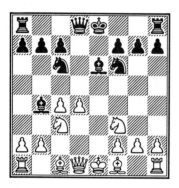

After 7.♗d2 ♕e7 (or 7...♗d2) we transpose to lines arising from 5.d4 ♗b4 6.♗d2, which are considered satisfactory for Black. On the other hand the text, which was unplayable in the <u>D11) 5.d4</u> line, has proved a tough nut for Black to crack. **7...♘e4** Black has also tried 7...♕e7 8.♗e3, with these examples:

1) 8...0-0-0 9.♗d3! (9.♗e2 ♘e4) 9...♗g4 10.0-0 ♗f3 11.♕f3 ♘d4 12.♗d4 ♖d4 13.♘b5 ♖dd8 14.a3 a6 15.♘c7 ♗d2 16.♖ad1 ±. Arkell–D. Olafsson, Reykjavic 1990.

2) 8...♗g4 9.♗e2 0-0-0 10.0-0 ♗c5 11.♘d5 ♘d5 12.cd5 ♖d5 13.♕b3

♗f3 14.♗f3 ♖d4 15.♗d4 ♗d4 16.♗c6 ± was Skripchenko–Lukasiewicz, Cannes Open 1997.

After 7...♘e4 play continues **8.♗d2** This move was impossible in the <u>D11) 5.d4</u> line because ...♕d4 would have been the reply. **8...♘d2 9.♕d2 ♕e7 10.0-0-0 0-0-0** No better is 10...0-0 11.a3 ♘a5 12.♔b1 ♗f5 13.♔a2 ♗c3 14.♕c3 b6 15.♗d3 ♕f6 16.♖he1 ♖fe8 17.h3 h6 18.♗f5 ♕f5 19.d5 ± Dolmatov–Boissonet, Buenos Aires 1991. **11.a3 ♗c5 12.d5 ♗g4 13.♖e1 ♕f8 14.b4 ♗f3 15.bc5 ♗h5 16.♕e3! ♘a5 17.♕h3 ♔b8 18.♕h5 ♕c5 19.♕e2 ♘b3 20.♔b2** Black had insufficient compensation for the piece in Hennigan–Stefansson, Oakham 1988 (although he ended up winning).

D122) 5...♕e7(!)

Because 5...♘c6 6.d4 was been such rough going for Black, this move has been gaining in popularity. **6.♕e2** After 6.♗e2 ♗c4 7.d3 ♗a6! 8.0-0, I like 8...♘c6 followed by 9...0-0-0 with strong pressure on White's d-pawn. Black played more cautiously in Kuczynski–Damaso, Debrecen 1992 with 8...♕d8 9.d4 ♗e7 10.♗a6 ♘a6 11.♘c3 c6 12.♖e1 0-0 13.♕b3 ♖b8 14.♗f4 ♗d6 15.♗g5 h6 16.♗h4, with chances for both sides. **6...♘c6 7.d4** Now play divides further:

→ **D1221) 7...0-0-0!?**
→ **D1222) 7...♗f5**
→ **D1223) 7...♗g4**

D1221) 7...0-0-0!? The sharpest treatment, which scored a brilliant win for Black in Minasian–Tu Hoang Thai, Yerevan Olympiad 1996. **8.d5** White can also seek safety by declining the offered piece with 8.♗e3 ♘e4 9.♘c3 ♗f5 10.0-0-0! ♘c3 11.bc3 ♕e4 12.♔b2 f6, △ 13...♘a5 ⩱ (Tu). **8...♕b4 9.♘c3** Forced, as after 9.♘bd2 ♗f5 the threat of 10...♖e8 is hard to answer. **9...♗f5 10.dc6!**

(see next diagram)

This is the critical test of 7...0-0-0. The actual game continued 10.♗e3

After 10.dc6!

♘e4 11.♖c1 g6! 12.a3 ♕a5 13.dc6 ♗g7 14.cb7 ♔b8 15.♘d2 ♗c3! 16.bc3 ♘d2 17.♗d2 ♖he8 18.♗e3 ♕a3 19.♖c2, and now instead of 19...♗e4? 20.♗a7? (20.♖d2 =) 20...♕a7 21.♖a2 ♗c2!, 0-1 Tu gives a clean win with 19...♖e6! 20.♖d2 ♕c3 21.♕d1 (21.c5? ♗g4! -+) 21...♖a6 22.♗e2 ♖a1 23.0-0 ♖d1 24.♖fd1 ♖d2 25.♖d2 ♗e4 -+. **10...♗c5 11.cb7 ♔b8 12.♗e3** Not 12.♘e5? ♕b7 13.♘f7 ♖de8 (Tu gave 13...♖he8 in his notes but missed 14.♘d8! +−) 14.♗e3 ♖hf8 15.♘g5 ♘g4 16.♘d5 ♘e3 (16...c6 17.♗c5! +−) 17.fe3 (17.♘e3? ♗b4) 17...c6 18.b4 ♗d6 19.♘c3 ♗b4 20.♖c1 ♕e7 21.♘f3 ♕e3 22.♕e3 ♖e3 23.♔d2 ♖c3 24.♖c3 ♖d8 ∓. **12...♘g4 13.♖d1** Surprisingly, 13.a3 ♕b6 14.♘d5 ♖d5! 15.cd5! ♗e3 16.fe3 ♘e3 17.♖c1 ♖e8 (−+ Tu) favors Black, as there is no stopping ...♗d7 and

♘-any regaining material. Black's Queen will start marauding the dark squares before White gets his Rooks coordinated. **13...♘e3 14.♖d8** Or 14.fe3 ♖d1 15.♔d1 ♖e8 16.♘d5 ♕b7 17.♕d2 c6 18.♕a5 ♗d6 19.♘f4 ♗g4 ⩲ (Tu). **14...♖d8 15.fe3 ♖e8 16.a3** Now Tu gives **16...♕b6 17.♘d5 ♕b3!** claiming "comp," but **18.♕d2 c6 19.♕c3!** repels the initiative, e.g. **19...♕a4 b4 +−**. If Black plays the immediate 16...♕b3!? the simple answer is 17.e4!, the point being that 17...♗a3 18.♘d4! works out in White's favor.

Unless Black has improvements, I am inclined to be skeptical of the piece sacrifice initiated by 7...0-0-0.

D1222) 7...♗f5 8.♕e7 ♗e7 9.a3! A suggestion by NM Bill Orton, to prevent ...♘b4. Inferior is 9.d5? ♘b4 10.♘a3 0-0-0 11.♘d4 ♗g6 12.♗e2 c6 = as in Grabics–A.Carvalho, Bratislava 1993 (by transposition). Or 11.♗e3 ♖he8 12.♘d4 (12.♗e2 ♘g4 13.♗a7?! ♗f6 ∓) 12...♗g6 13.♗e2 ♗c5! ⩲. **9...0-0-0** No better is 9...♗g4 10.♘bd2 0-0-0 11.d5 ♗f3 12.♘f3 ♘a5 13.♗e3 ♘b3 14.♖d1 ±. **10.♗e3** White needs to catch up in development before pushing pawns: 10.d5 ♘a5 11.♘d4 ♗g6

12.b4 (Or 12.♗e3 c5! 13.dc6 ♖d4! 14.cb7 ♔b7 15.♗d4 ♘b3 −+) gives Black the winning shot 12...♘d5! 13.cd5 (13.ba5 ♗f6 14.cd5 ♗d4 15.♖a2 ♖he8 −+) 13...♗f6 14.♗e3 ♗d4 15.♗d4 ♘b3 −+, with a huge Black initiative. **10...♖he8 11.♘bd2** Again, premature is 11.d5 ♘a5 12.♘bd2 ♗c5 13.b4 ♗e3 14.fe3 ♖e3 15.♔f2 ♘b3! ∓. **11...♘g4 12.h3 ♘e3 13.fe3 ♗f6 14.♔f2** White has consolidated, and Black's compensation for the gambit pawn is more elusive than ever.

D1223) 7...♗g4 8.♕e7 Another suggestion by Orton is 8.♗e3!. By keeping Queens on the board, White deprives Black of counter-play based on ...♘b4-c2. After 8...0-0-0 9.d5 ♘e5 10.♘c3 ♖e8, White can try to force matters:

11.c5!? ♕d8 12.c6 (12.♕b5 ♗f3 13.c6 ♘c6 14.gf3 ♘e5 ∓) 12...♗c5 13.♕b5 ♗b6 ∞ 14.♘e5

♖e5 15.h3 ♗f5 16.♗e2 ♘d5 17.♗d4 ♗d3! 18.cb7 ♔b8 19.♕d3 ♘f4 20.♕f3 ♕d4 21.0-0 ♘e2 22.♘e2 ♕b2 23.♘g3 ♖e6 =. This is all highly unclear and needs practical tests. White's best from the diagram seems to be 11.0-0-0 ♕b4 12.♕c2! ±, △ 12...♘c4? 13.♗c4 ♕c4 14.♖d4 ♕a6 15.♖a4 +- (Orton). Returning to 8.♕e7, we have **8...♗e7 9.♗e3**

9...♗f3 Equally complex and playable is 9...0-0-0 10.d5 ♘b4 11.♘a3 c6. For example:

1) 12.♗a7? ♖he8 13.0-0-0 ♗f5! 14.b3 ♘e4 15.♖e1 cd5 16.cd5 ♘c6!! -+ leaves White is exposed to a strong attack.

2) 12.♗e2 cd5 and now instead of 13.0-0 ♔b8 14.♘b5 a6 15.♗f4 ♔a8 = as in Frois–Almeida, Almada 1988, White gets a minuscule edge with 13.cd5 ♘fd5 14.♗a7 ♘f4 15.♖c1 ♘c6 16.♔f1 ♘e2

17.♔e2 ♗f6 18.♘b5 ♗b2 19.♖c2 ♗f6 20.♗e3 ±.

3) 12.♘e5!? ♖he8! 13.h3 (13.♘f7 ♘bd5! 14.♘c2 ♘b4 15.♘a3 =; 13.♗e2 ♗e2 14.♔e2 ♗f8! 15.♘f7 ♖d7 16.♘g5 cd5 17.cd5 ♖d5 18.♘f3 ♘d3, △ 19...♘b2 or 19...♘f2! ∓) 13...♘h5 14.g4 ♗c5! 15.♗c5 ♖e5 16.♗e3 ♗g6 17.dc6 bc6 18.♗g2 h5 19.gh5 ♗h5 20.♔f1 ±. Black has some compensation for the pawn, but probably not enough.

After 9...♗f3 from the last diagram play continues **10.gf3 0-0-0 11.d5 ♘b4 12.♘a3 ♘d7 13.♗h3** Black does not seem to have quite enough for the pawn:

1) **13...♗f6 14.0-0-0 ♘a2 15.♔b1 ♘b4 16.♗a7 b6 17.d6! ±.**

2) **13...♘d3 14.♔e2 ♘b2 15.♘b5! a6 16.♘a7 ♔b8 17.♖hb1 ♗f6 18.♖b2! ♗b2 19.♖b1 ♘b6 20.♖b2 ♔a7 21.d6 ♖d6 22.c5 ♖c6 23.cb6 cb6 24.a4 a5 25.♖b5 ♔a6 26.♗f5 +-** was Soylu–C.P. Santos, European Cup 1997.

3) **13...♔b8 14.♔f1 ♗f6 15.♖b1 ♘e5 16.f4 ♘ed3 17.♗f5 g6 18.♗d3 ♘d3 19.b4 ±.**

3.♘f3; 3.♗b5; 3.♘c3; 3.c4

I cannot fully justify the Icelandic Gambit, but those who are addicted to attacking play may like to take their chances with it. They may also want to avoid defending a Caro-Kann, the usual outcome of 3...c6.

D2) 3...c6 4.dc6(?) ♘c6

This is the Scandinavian Gambit, which White rarely accepts as it ensures both his d-pawn and development will be backward. Of course, 4.d4 cd5 is the Panov-Botvinnik variation of the Caro-Kann. After the text we consider:

→ D21) 5.♘f3?!
→ D22) 5.d3

D21) 5.♘f3 e5 Now play divides further:

→ D211) 6.♘c3?
→ D212) 6.d3

D211) 6.♘c3? e4 7.♘g5 ♗f5 8.f3 Or 8.♗e2 h6 9.♘h3 g5 10.g4? ♗g6 11.♕a4 ♗d6 12.♘d5 0-0 13.f4 ef3 14.♗f3 ♘d5 15.cd5 ♖e8 16.♔f2 ♘b4, 0-1 as in Kosulejeva–Gaprindashvili, USSR 1960. 8...♗c5 9.fe4 0-0! 10.d3 10.ef5 ♖e8 11.♗e2 (11.♘e2 ♕d4 12.♘h3 ♘e5! 13.d3 ♗b4 −+) 11...♕d4 12.♘h3 (12.♕a4 ♕f2 13.♔d1 ♕g2 14.♗f3 ♕g5 15.d4 ♕f5 −+; 12.♖f1 ♕h4 13.g3 ♕h2 ∓) 12...♕h4 13.♔f1 ♖e5 14.♗f3 ♖ae8 −+ (Silman and Grefe). 10...♖e8 11.♗f4 h6 12.♘f3 ♘g4 13.♗g3 ♘b4 14.♘d5 ♗e4! 15.de4 ♖e4 16.♗e2 ♕a5 −+ The crunchy finish to Zentai–Tiszay, corr. 1951 was 17.♘c3 ♖d8 18.♕a4 ♘d3 19.♔f1 ♘e3 20.♔g1 ♘c4 21.♔f1 ♘e3 22.♔g1 ♖a4, 0-1.

D212) 6.d3

6...e4! 7.de4 7.♕e2 ♗b4 8.♗d2 0-0 9.de4 ♘e4 10.♗b4 ♖e8! −+

Emms; 7.♘g5 ♗b4 8.♘c3 ♗g4 ∓ was Maksudov–Mergelishvili, USSR 1961. **7...♕d1 8.♔d1 ♘e4 9.♗e3 ♗f5 10.♘h4 0-0-0 11.♔c1** Instead, 11.♔e2 ♗e6 12.♔f3 (12.b3 g5 13.♘f3 ♗g7) 12...f5 13.g4 ♘e5 14.♔f4 g5! 15.♔e5 ♗d6 16.♔d4 (16.♔e6 ♖he8 17.♔f7 ♖e7#) 16...♗c7#, 0-1 was Holzmann–Kaspar, corr. 1980. **11...♗e6 12.♘c3 ♘c3 13.bc3 b6 14.♘f3 ♗c5 15.♗c5 bc5 16.♖b1 ♖he8 17.♗e2 ♗h3! 18.gh3 ♖e2 19.♖b2 ♖b2 20.♔b2 ♖d3 21.♘g5 ♖d2** with a winning endgame for Black in Chandler–Adams, Hastings 1989/90.

D22) 5.d3 e5 6.♘c3 ♗f5 Or 6...♗c5 7.♗e3 ♗e3 8.fe3 ♕b6 9.♕d2 ♗e6 10.e4 ♘g4! 11.♘d5 ♗d5 12.cd5 ♘d4 with compensation (Grefe and Silman). **7.♘f3 ♕d7**

Transparent and good. Boleslavsky's 7...♗b4 8.♗e2 e4 is unclear at best after 9.♘h4 ♗e6 10.0-0 ed3 11.♗d3 ♗c3 12.bc3 ♘e5 13.♗f5!? (13.♗e2 ♕d1 14.♖d1 ♖c8 15.f4!, Minev) 13...♗c4 14.♕d4! 0-0 15.♕e5 ♗f1 16.♔f1 ♕d1 17.♕e1 ♕h5 18.g3 ♖fe8 19.♗e3 g5 20.h3 ♖e5 (20...gh4? 21.g4) 21.♕b1 ±; or 13...0-0 14.♕e2 ♘fg4 15.♗e6 fe6 16.♘f3 ♘f3 17.gf3 ♘f6 18.♕e6, and White's surfeit of pawns and active play make up for any cosmetic defects in his position. **8.♗e2 0-0-0 9.0-0 ♗d3 10.♗d3 ♕d3 11.♕a4 ♗c5 12.♗g5 ♕g6!** Grefe and Silman offered this as an improvement over Lasker's 12...h6 13.♗f6 gf6 14.♘d5, which favors White. **13.♕b5** Or 13.♗f6 gf6 14.♕b5 ♗d6, △ 15...♖hg8 and ...f5 with good play for Black. **13...e4! 14.♘e5 ♕g5 15.♘c6 a6!** A finesse to take away a Queen check at b5. **16.♕a4 bc6 17.♕c6 ♔b8 −+** Black is winning (analysis by Grefe and Silman).

Acknowledgments

Thanks to IM John Donaldson, whose article in *Inside Chess* inspired this work, for useful input along the way; to database wizard Maj. Bill Wall, USAF; to GM John Fedorowicz for sharing an important game score; to NM Bill Orton for helpful analysis of the Icelandic gambit; and to NM Sid Pickard, for supplying the initial motivation for this project as well as useful analytical help.

About the Author

Selby Anderson was born in Baton Rouge, Louisiana on March 11, 1955. He graduated *summa cum laude* in 1977 from Trinity University at San Antonio, where he lives, taking degrees in Economics and Philosophy. After completing his studies, Anderson turned his attention to chess and gained the National Master title in 1985. At that time he took over as editor of *Texas Knights*, the official chess publication of that state, guiding it to become a top quality magazine. Anderson, who maintains an Elo rating of 2300, has placed 1st or 2nd in several strong regional tournaments, making him a formidible opponent at any level of competition. His other interests include opera, which he indulges by singing with the San Antonio Symphony Chorus, and acting, having once performed the lead part in *Mikado*.

Index of Variations

<u>Chapter Three</u>
1.e4 d5 2.ed5 ♘f6 3.d4 ♗g4
4.♘f3 ♛d5

Bibliography

This list amounts to a complete bibliography of the Center Counter Defense. Readers wishing to do further research, build a Center Counter library, or simply be made aware of the literature on this opening will find here a valuable reference.

Bekemann, Uwe. Die Skandinavischen Gambits. Dresden: Manfred Madler, 1995.

du Mont, J. Chess Openings Illustrated: The Centre Counter. London: George Bell & Sons, 1919.

Dunne, Alex and David Taylor. Center Counter Uprising: Main Line Mieses. Davenport: Thinker's Press, 1990.

Edwards, R.B. The Scandinavian Defence: Book I, The Modern Variation. London (Canada): CCCP, 1987.

Emms, John. The Scandinavian. Brighton: The Chess Press, 1997.

Fries Nielsen and Niels Jorgen. Skandinavisk. Brabrand: Skakcentralens forlag, 1982.

Ganzo, Julio. La defensa Alekhine y la defensa escandinava. Madrid: Ricardo Aguilera, 1957.

Grefe, John and Jeremy Silman. Center Counter. Coraopolis: Chess Enterprises, 1983.

Hall, John. Let's Play the Center Counter Game. Dallas: Chess Digest, 1972.

Harmon, R. and Shaun Talbot. Winning with the Scandinavian. London: Batsford, 1993.

Hodges, P. Center Counter. Hagerstown: R & D Publishing, 1994.

Jonsson, Bo. Skandinaviskt Parti. Uppsala: Schackbulletins forlag, 1967.

Keene, Raymond and David Levy. A Reportoire for the Attacking Player. London: Batsford, 1994.

Lhoste, R. La defense scandinave. Paris: Shakmatny Bulletin, 1965.

Lutes, John W. Scandinavian Defense, Anderssen Counter Attack. Coraopolis: Chess Enterprises, 1992.

Martin, Andrew, ed. Trends: Scandinavian Defence. Brighton: Trends Publication, 1991.

Mieses, Jacques. Drei Aufsatze...die Skandinavische Partie. Berlin: Bernard Kagan, 1918.

Moravsky, N., ed. Skandinavska: B01 2...Dd8xd5. Olomouc: Sachova Caissa, 1994.

Pytel, K. Skandinavisch, 1.e4 d5. Munster: Munster International, 1990.

Smith, Ken and John Hall. Winning with the Center Counter. Dallas: Chess Digest, 1991.

Tesh, R. ed. The Center Counter Game: Rehabilitated. Dallas: Chess Digest, 1980.

Varnusz, Egon. Skandinavisches Gambit und die Panow Variante. Frankfurt: Harri Deutsch, 1993.

Varnusz, Egon, et al. Skandinavisch. Mannheim: Reinhold Dreier, 1992.

Magazines

Donaldson, John. "New Paths in the Center Counter: The Portuguese Variation," Inside Chess. vol.9 nr.16, p.20.

Spraggett, Kevin. "The Portuguese Variation of the Scandinavian Defense," En Passant. nr.143, April 1997.

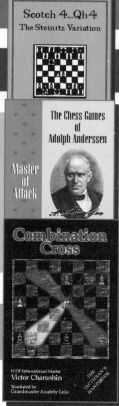